MW00443983

AWS CERTIFIED CLOUD PRACTITIONER STUDY GUIDE:

THE ULTIMATE CHEAT SHEET PRACTICE EXAM.

QUESTIONS WITH ANSWERS & DETAILED EXPLANATIONS FOR THE LATEST CLF-C01 EXAM

Barry Adams

© **Copyright 2019 - All rights reserved.**

The content contained within this book may not be reproduced, duplicated or transmitted without direct written permission from the author or the publisher.

Under no circumstances will any blame or legal responsibility be held against the publisher, or author, for any damages, reparation, or monetary loss due to the information contained within this book. Either directly or indirectly.

Legal Notice:

This book is copyright protected. This book is only for personal use. You cannot amend, distribute, sell, use, quote or paraphrase any part, or the content within this book, without the consent of the author or publisher.

Disclaimer Notice:

Please note the information contained within this document is for educational and entertainment purposes only. All effort has been executed to present accurate, up to date, and reliable, complete information. No warranties of any kind are declared or implied. Readers acknowledge that the author is not engaging in the rendering of legal, financial, medical or professional advice. The content within this book has been derived from various sources. Please consult a licensed professional before attempting any techniques outlined in this book.

By reading this document, the reader agrees that under no circumstances is the author responsible for any losses, direct or indirect, which are incurred as a result of the use of information

contained within this document, including, but not limited to, —
errors, omissions, or inaccuracies.

Table Of Contents

AWS CERTIFIED CLOUD PRACTITIONER STUDY GUIDE...1

Introduction: 6

Cloud Concepts...13

Security.. 26

Technology 40

Billing and Pricing 56

AWS Services 72

How to Secure Your AWS Resources 79

Conclusion.. 87

Answers to Review Questions 91

AWS CERTIFIED SOLUTIONS ARCHITECT ASSOCIATE STUDY GUIDE...138

Introduction: 139

Compute...143

Storage...153

Networking...162

Content delivery 174

Databases...183

Analytics 196

Application Integration 207

AWS Security, Identity & Compliance 219

Network Architectures **225**

Conclusion **233**

Answers to Review Questions **237**

Introduction:

I am addicted to certification! I have been receiving I.T. certifications for over 18 years, have passed 50+ exams during this period, and have failed only twice for one exam. I will explain how to pass the AWS certification exams the first time.

The key to passing the AWS certification exams is simply preparing correctly. Preparation includes the following five steps that I will explain in this post:

- Practice (practice)

- Training (mainly online video)

- Theory (read)

- Practical questions

- Take the test

Many companies also sell different resources to prepare you for exams. Still, the material's quality can vary widely, so it's worth paying attention to what you use.

BACKGROUND OF THE INVESTIGATION

Many people who take these exams have the necessary computer skills. It may be much more difficult for you if you are a newcomer and cannot distinguish a block from an object store or container virtual machine. That said, you don't need to have excellent skills in the underlying technologies that support AWS since cloud computing removes much of that complexity.

In the exam plan, AWS makes the following recommendations for AWS-specific knowledge and experience.

The exam recently changed the format this year. The following image shows the differences between the new and old form (this applies to all AWS certification exams at the corresponding level).

AWS technology is evolving incredibly fast, so I would recommend using the latest exam format if you start your studies now as it will better match the features available today. It is not as generous as the more incredible difficulty of some of the questions on the new exam. But don't be discouraged, the accompanying exams aren't too tricky, and you have plenty of resources to prepare.

STEP 1: IT ALL BEGINS WITH PRACTICE

One of the keys to learning technology is to play with it. Don't worry if you don't work with AWS. Not everyone can work with the technologies they study in a professional context, and indeed, I have passed many exams without real work experience.

AWS allows you to create an account for free, and the free tier will enable you to use specific AWS services for free.

The free tier offers many free services every month, including (among others):

Free AWS tier: It's a great way to gain experience, and you can take things out and take them apart without costing you a penny. It's amazing what you can do on the free tier for a whole year!

STEP 2: ONLINE VIDEO TRAINING

Online video training is an excellent tool. There are many AWS certification courses online that allow you to relax and absorb everything.

Classes can range from PowerPoint to highly lab-oriented, and this is where the problem of their isolated Use lies. Courses with a lot of content can be very dry and dull, and more practical terms will be light and will help you get ready to take the exam.

To make sure you pass the exam and gain hands-on experience on AWS for the first time, sign up for the latest AWS Certified cloud practioner hands-on video training in digital cloud training.

STEP 3: THEORY

Some people find it boring, but there is no substitute for theory, and there is still plenty to read. I like to practice a lot of I.T. before getting caught up in the theoretical part that helps things make sense (and keeps it interesting). It is essential to keep practicing as you gain more knowledge: use it or lose it!

The AWS website contains a wealth of information, so you can use it pretty much if you want. There are books and e-books, too, but things are changing rapidly in the AWS world and are generally updated with time.

My strategy in learning theory is to take lots of notes. When I look at the online courses, I also pay attention to the essential facts. Having concise and summary training notes becomes invaluable when you try to remember thousands of points because you can come back to them at any time without having to read long articles. Try a digital note-taking tool like Microsoft OneNote or Evernote.

STEP 4: PRACTICAL QUESTION

Using high-quality, practical questions will help you understand the types of questions you may encounter during the exam and identify weaknesses.

However, the challenge is to find excellent quality practice questions. There have always been many exams on the Internet, and various companies have low-quality questions (which they generally copy between themselves).

Remember that AWS changes quickly, so questions must be current. I want to avoid common or expired problems!

I suggest that you test multiple times during your preparation, don't wait for the exam time. The practical questions should be considered both a learning tool and an assessment tool and should be used from the beginning.

STEP 5: EXAM TIME

Another key to my success in I.T. certification exams is that I have never booked the exam before. I am sure I am ready. You should receive 80 to 90% of the practical questions just before you think about booking.

The actual pass rate is much lower than this. Still, there will always be surprises during the day with technologies that you haven't covered enough during training.

Once you've trained, taken a course, viewed my training notes, and passed the training questions, you're ready to go. If you prepared well, you don't have to get crowded at the last minute, so get rid of all the stress and come back.

Try to read each question first and see the answers. You can develop talent for this and often quickly discover what the answer will be. Go back to the problem in detail and make sure you haven't forgotten anything before choosing.

Some questions are an objective, a multiple choice with multiple answers, and you may need to select "all that apply." Make sure you are not mistaken, as it is an easy mistake to make!

AWS certification exams are reasonably well written, so there are generally not many confusing questions. If you have prepared high-quality, practical questions to prepare yourself, you will need to be well equipped to handle everything. Good study and good luck with your exams!

Domain 1: Cloud Concepts 26%

Domain 2: Security and Compliance 25%

Domain 3: Technology 33%

Domain 4: Billing and Pricing 16%

TOTAL 100%

Domain 1: Cloud Concepts

1.1.Define the AWS Cloud and its value proposition

1.2 Identify aspects of AWS Cloud economics

1.3 List the different cloud architecture design principles

Domain 2: Security and Compliance

2.1 Define the AWS shared responsibility model

2.2 Define AWS Cloud security and compliance concepts

2.3 Identify AWS access management capabilities

2.4 Identify resources for security support

Domain 3: Technology

3.1 Define methods of deploying and operating in the AWS Cloud

3.2 Define the AWS global infrastructure

3.3 Identify the core AWS services

3.4 Identify resources for technology support

Domain 4: Billing and Pricing

4.1 Compare and contrast the various pricing models for AWS

4.2 Recognize the different account structures about AWS billing and pricing

4.3 Identify resources available for billing support

Cloud Concepts

Setting up your own data center is time-consuming and costly: skilled personnel must acquire and maintain. Also, you can never scale as needed. After all, your company should grow, and therefore your I.T. must always be one step ahead. For this reason, you often provide more resources than the employees currently need. After all, a functioning data center is vital for most companies. If it fails, the work stops. And nobody can afford that, so you have to spend too much rather than too little at the data center.

With cloud computing, you go a different way: Instead of purchasing, installing, and maintaining the technology yourself, you can use web services. In most cases, this form of modern outsourcing runs through a rental model. Capacities can be quickly booked in this way - and promptly when you need them.

What is Cloud Computing?

In principle, cloud computing is only a collective term: This describes the offer of hardware and software over the Internet. It does not specify the extent to which the services must be provided - from simple cloud storage, in which users receive storage capacity on remote servers in addition to their own hard disk space, to the infrastructure in the cloud, through which companies have complete data centers via the Internet Respectively.

Definition of cloud computing

On-demand self-service: It should be possible for users to independently request the required resources without having to contact an employee of the provider each time.

Broad Network Access: Access to cloud computing works over the Internet. No unusual techniques or protocols may be used. The Use of standardized methods ensures that all users have easy access to the service.

Resource pooling: The merging of several computing instances is the essential prerequisite for cloud computing. Such pools are usually used in the form of server farms to supply several users with computing power or storage capacity at the same time. It is rarely apparent to the customer which device he is using: The accommodations are allocated dynamically.

Rapid elasticity: The delivery of capacities has to be quick and needs-based. At best, automatisms are active that switch resources on or off without customers' or employees' help.

Measured Service: The Use of the cloud offer is monitored at all times. It creates more transparency for both the provider and the user.

Deployment Models

The deployment models describe the type of offer: Are instances reserved for only one user or company, or do you share the pool with other people? The deployment model results from the answer to this question.

Community Cloud: The Community Cloud works in a similar way to a private cloud, but with this model, several customers share a dedicated

14

hardware instance. The users' users' composition is not chosen at random. Still, several customers - mostly from the same business area or with similar interests - come together in a targeted manner. The Community Cloud can also be managed either in a company or externally. The goal is to achieve savings compared to multiple private clouds.

Public cloud: This type of provision corresponds to the basic idea behind a cloud. A server network is used together with the general public. Who uses which hardware is not visible to the user and cannot be determined by him.

Hybrid cloud: This is a hybrid of the two models of the private and public clouds. A company or a remote user decides to leave a specific part of the operation (e.g., security-related aspects) in the intimate environment and choose the public cloud for other details.

It is cloud computing.

You can also rent I.T. Most of these I.T. services providers are geographically distant. Hence, the data and applications are no longer on your company's local computer but in the cloud. It just means that your information is no longer stored directly with you, but away from the company center. And only you. The advantages are more flexibility, scalability, and low costs since there is no separate server structure.

Do you think that is not the case with you? Not correct! As soon as you have an e-mail address on the Internet, enter your username and password there; you are a cloud provider user. Other examples would be:

- Dropbox

- Microsoft OneDrive

- Google Drive

- Amazon Drive

- iCloud

However, when choosing your "cloud provider," you should make sure that all relevant security regulations are met. By the way, the world's world's strictest security requirements apply in Germany, which is why many companies choose a cloud "Made in Germany."

REVIEW QUESTIONS

Question 1

Which items can be configured from within the VPC management console? (Select TWO.)

1. Regions

2. Load Balancing

3. Security Groups

4. Subnets

5. Auto Scaling

Question 2

Which benefit of the AWS Cloud eliminates the need for users to try estimating future infrastructure usage?

1. Economies of scale

2. Easy global deployments

3. Security of the AWS Cloud

4. The elasticity of the AWS Cloud

Question 3

Which AWS support plan should you use if you need a response time of < 15 minutes for a business-critical system failure?

1. Basic

2. Developer

3. Business

4. Enterprise

Question 4

Under the shared responsibility model, what are examples of shared controls? (Select TWO.)

1. Storage system patching

2. Physical and environmental

3. Patch management

4.   Service and Communications Protection

5.   Configuration management

Question 5

Which feature of AWS allows you to deploy a new application for which the requirements may change over time?

1.   Elasticity

2.   Fault tolerance

3.   High availability

4.   Disposable resources

Question 6

Which of the statements below is accurate regarding Amazon S3 buckets? (Select TWO.)

1.   Bucket names must be unique regionally

2.   Bucket names must be unique globally

3.   Buckets are replicated globally

4.   Buckets are region-specific

5.   Buckets can contain other buckets

Question 7

The AWS global infrastructure is composed of? (Select TWO.)

1.   Clusters

2.   I.P. Subnets

3.   Fault Zones

4.   Availability Zones

5.   Regions

Question 8

A company stores copies of backups on Amazon S3 and requires rapid access but low resiliency. Which storage class is optimized for these requirements?

1.   Amazon S3 Glacier

2.   Amazon S3 One Zone-Infrequent Access

3.   Amazon S3 Standard

4.   Amazon S3 Glacier Deep Archive

Question 9

What is the term for describing the action of automatically running scripts on Amazon EC2 instances when launched to install software?

1.   Workflow Automation

2.   Bootstrapping

3.   Golden Images

4.   Containerization

Question 10

Which service can be used for building and integrating loosely-coupled, distributed applications?

1.   Amazon EFS

2.   Amazon RDS

3.   Amazon EBS

4.   Amazon SNS

Question 11

Which AWS service allows you to connect to storage from on-premise servers using standard file protocols?

1.   Amazon Glacier

2.   Amazon EFS

3.   Amazon EBS

4.   Amazon S3

Question 12

Which service allows you to run code as functions without needing to provision or manage servers?

1.   AWS Lambda

2.   Amazon EC2

3.   AWS CodeDeploy

4.   Amazon EKS

Question 13

To transfer a website to one type of Cloud while its brochure is on another, which Cloud can be used?

A. Real Cloud

B. Private Cloud

C. Dynamic Cloud

D. Hybrid Cloud

Question 14

When public and private cloud services are mixed, the Cloud formed will be?

A. Private Cloud

B. Public Cloud

C. Real Cloud

D. Hybrid Cloud

Question 15

What are the advantages of having infrastructure hosted on the AWS Cloud? Choose two answers:

A. Having the pay as you go, model,

B. Having complete control over the physical infrastructure

C. zero Upfront costs

D. No need to worry about security

Question 16

When instantiating compute resources, what are two techniques for using automated, repeatable processes that are fast and avoid human error? (Select TWO.)

1.   Performance monitoring

2.   Fault tolerance

3.   Snapshotting

4.   Infrastructure as code

5.   Bootstrapping

Question 17

What strategy can assist with allocating metadata to AWS resources for cost tracking and visibility?

1.   Access Control

2.   Categorizing

3.   Labeling

4.   Tagging

Question 18

What is the scope of a VPC within a region?

1.   Spans all Availability Zones within the region

2.   Spans all Availability Zones globally

3.   At least two subnets per region

4.   At least 2 data centers per region

Question 19

Which AWS service is primarily used for software version control?

1.   AWS CodeDeploy

2.   AWS Cloud9

3.   AWS CodeStar

4.   AWS CodeCommit

Question 20

What benefits does Amazon EC2 provide over using non-cloud servers? (Select TWO.)

1.   Complete control of the hypervisor layer

2.   Fault tolerance

3.   High-availability with an SLA of 99.999%

4.   Inexpensive

5.   Elastic web-scale computing

Question 21

Which service allows you to expand and shrink your application in response to demand automatically?

1. Amazon EC2 Auto Scaling

2. Amazon DynamoDB

3. AWS ElastiCache

4. Amazon Elastic Load Balancing

Question 22

Which architectural best practice aims to reduce the interdependencies between services?

1. Automation

2. Removing Single Points of Failure

3. Loose Coupling

4. Services, Not Servers

Question 23

An architect wants to find a tool for consistently deploying the same resources through a templated configuration. Which AWS service can be used?

1. AWS CloudFormation

2. AWS Elastic Beanstalk

3. AWS CodeBuild

4. AWS CodeDeploy

Question 24

A company has an application with users in both Australia and Germany. All the company infrastructure is currently provisioned in the Europe (Frankfurt) Region, and Australian users are experiencing high latency.

What should the company do to reduce latency?

1.   Launch additional Amazon EC2 instances in Frankfurt to handle the demand

2.   Use AWS Transit Gateway to route users from Australia to the application quickly

3.   Implement AWS Direct Connect for users in Australia

4.   Provision resources in the Asia Pacific (Sydney) Region in Australia

Question 25

Which of the following is a principle of good AWS Cloud architecture design?

1. Implement loose coupling

2. Implement vertical scaling

3. Implement single points of failure

4. Implement monolithic design

Security

Security is regarded as the highest priority service of AWS. As a user of AWS services, you will be gaining profit from a data center and a network architecture, which has been built to meet all the requirements of the highest organizations, which are security-sensitive. While using the cloud, securing it from all possible sides is of utter importance. Cloud security is somewhat like the security of your on-premises data center. It is of much more critical than the cost of the hardware and maintenance facilities. You are not required to manage the storage devices or physical servers in the cloud. Instead of doing it yourself, you use security tools based on software to protect and monitor the overall flow of information that goes in and out of the cloud resources. It can be done while maintaining a super-secure environment without paying for those services that you do not use at all. It means that you can enjoy premium security and that too at a lesser cost when compared to the protection of your on-premises data center environment. While using AWS's services, you need to inherit all the practices regarding AWS policies, operational processes, and architecture, which have been built for satisfying the ultimate requirements of those customers who are the most security-sensitive. You can enjoy the agility along with flexibility with security services from AWS for your data centers. AWS Cloud comes with a shared responsibility model. While AWS manages the cloud's security, you are the one who is entirely responsible for the security in the cloud. In simple words, you can retain the security control which you choose for protecting your content, applications, platform, networks, and systems in the same way that you would have done for an on-premises data center. You will also receive the required guidance and competence via online personnel, resources, and partners. AWS provides users with various advisories for current issues. You can also enjoy working along with AWS whenever you come across any security issue. To meet up with your cloud security objectives, you also get access to various features and tools. AWS provides the users with tools and features specific to security across network configuration, access control, management, and encryption of data. The AWS environments are audited at regular intervals with certifications from various accreditation bodies across verticals and geographies. You can take full advantage of the automated tools in the AWS environment for access reporting and asset inventory.

Benefits of AWS Security

·   AWS security comes with various benefits that can make your cloud working much more convenient and secure. The infrastructure of AWS puts in place robust safeguards for protecting the privacy of the users. All of your data is stored in super-secure data centers of AWS.

·   You can meet compliance requirements with AWS security. AWS is known for managing various programs of compliance within its infrastructure. In simple words, the segments of your required submission have been completed already.

·   You can save lots of money with AWS security services. You can cut down your costs with the help of AWS data centers. You can maintain the highest security standards without any need to manage your facility.

- You can scale quickly and conveniently with AWS security services. The security services also scale with the usage of your AWS Cloud. Whatever your business's size, the infrastructure of AWS has been designed to keep all your data safe.

The Shared Responsibility Model

Responsibility on the part of AWS: Security of the Cloud

AWS is solely responsible for the overall protection of its infrastructure that runs all the services offered in the AWS cloud. The infrastructure consists of software, hardware, networking along with all the facilities that run the benefits of AWS cloud. Responsibility on the part of the customer: Security in the Cloud

The obligation on the customer's interest is determined by the services of the AWS cloud selected by the customer. It ultimately determines the overall amount of configuration work that the customer needs to perform as a part of the security responsibilities. For instance, any service of AWS such as Amazon EC2 or Elastic Compute Cloud is being categorized as IaaS or Infrastructure as a Service and requires performance on the part of the customer regarding all the necessary management tasks and configuration of security. Customers who deploy EC2 instance from Amazon are liable for the complete management of the guest O.S. or operating system that also includes the security and update patches, configuration of the firewall provided by AWS, which is known as a security group, and any application utilities or software which is being installed by the customer on the EC2 instances.

For AWS's abstracted services such as DynamoDB or Amazon S3, the infrastructure layer is operated by AWS and the platforms. The customers can easily access the endpoints to retrieve and store the data. The customers are solely responsible for managing their data, including the options of encryption, classification of the assets, and Use of IAM tools for application of the required permissions.

This AWS and customer shared responsibility model also extends itself to the I.T. controls. Like AWS and its customers share the responsibility of the I.T. environment's operations, the operation, management, and verification of the I.T. controls are also shared between the two. AWS can help the customers by relieving the customers' burden to operate the controls by managing all the required rules associated with the infrastructure, which is deployed in the environment of AWS that might have been driven by the AWS customers.

Monitoring And Logging Features

AWS security provides you with various features and tools to have a complete visualization of what is happening in AWS's environment. It also includes:

• Options for log aggregation, compliance reporting, and streamlining the investigations.

• Usage of AWS CloudTrail for having deep visibility into the API calls that also include who, when, what, and where all the needs were made.

29

- Alert notifications with the help of Amazon CloudWatch whenever thresholds exceed or any specific event occurs.

Identify And Access Management.

AWS security services offer you all the capabilities for defining, managing, and enforcing user access policies across all AWS services. It also includes:

- AWS IAM or Identity and Access Management for determining the respective user account with proper permissions across AWS's resources.

- AWS Directory Service allows you to federate and integrate with the various corporate directories to improve end-user experience and reduce the overhead of administration.

- AWS Multi-Factor Authentication for all the privileged accounts and options for the authenticators based on hardware.

REVIEW QUESTIONS

Question 1:

Under the AWS shared responsibility model, what are the customer's responsibilities? (Select TWO.)

1.   Physical network devices, including firewalls

2.   Physical and environmental security

3.   Security of data in transit

4.   Data integrity authentication

5.   Storage device decommissioning

Question 2:

According to the AWS shared responsibility model, what are the controls that customers fully inherit from AWS? (Choose two)

A. Communications controls.

B. Environmental controls.

C. Patch Management.

D. Resource Configuration Management.

E. Physical controls.

Question 3:

Which feature can you use to grant read/write access to an Amazon S3 bucket?

1.   IAM Role

2.   IAM User

3.   IAM Policy

4.   IAM Group

Question 4:

Which aspects of security on AWS are customer responsibilities? (Select TWO.)

1.   Setting up account password policies

2.   Patching of storage systems

3.   Server-side encryption

4.   Availability of AWS regions

5.   Physical access controls

Question 5:

Which AWS service is used to enable multi-factor authentication?

1.   Amazon STS

2.   AWS KMS

3.   AWS IAM

4.   Amazon EC2

Question 6:

Under the AWS shared responsibility model, what is the customer responsible for? (Select TWO.)

1.   Physical security of the data center

2.   Patch management of infrastructure

3.   Encryption of customer data

4.   Configuration of security groups

5.   Replacement and disposal of disk drives

Question 7:

Which services are involved with security? (Select TWO.)

1. AWS DMS

2. AWS KMS

3. AWS CloudHSM

4. AWS SMS

5. Amazon ELB

Question 8:

Which of the following should be used to improve the security of access to the AWS Management Console? (Select TWO.)

1. Security group rules

2. AWS Multi-Factor Authentication (AWS MFA)

3. Strong password policies

4. AWS Secrets Manager

5. AWS Certificate Manager

Question 9:

How can an organization assess application for vulnerabilities and deviations from best practice?

1. Use AWS WAF

2. Use AWS Shield

3. Use AWS Inspector

4.   Use AWS Artifact

Question 10:

Which AWS service gives you centralized control over the encryption keys used to protect your data?

1.   AWS STS

2.   Amazon EBS

3.   AWS KMS

4.   AWS DMS

Question 11:

Which AWS service protects against common exploits that could compromise application availability, compromise security or consume excessive resources?

1.   Security Group

2.   Network ACL

3.   AWS Shield

4.   AWS WAF

Question 12:

Which IAM entity can be used for assigning permissions to multiple users?

1.   IAM Group

2.   IAM User

3.   IAM Role

4.   IAM password policy

Question 13:

Which IAM entity can be used for assigning permissions to AWS services?

1.   Security Token Service (STS)

2.   IAM Policy

3.   IAM Role

4.   IAM Access Key ID and Secret Access Key

Question 14:

Which IAM entity is associated with an access key I.D. and secret access key?

1.   IAM Group

2.   IAM User

3.   IAM Role

4.   IAM Policy

Question 15:

How can an organization track resource inventory and configuration history for security and regulatory compliance?

1.   Run a report with AWS Artifact

2.   Create an Amazon CloudTrail trail

3.   Configure AWS Config with the resource types

4.   Implement Amazon GuardDuty

Question 16:

Which AWS service provides on-demand downloads of AWS security and compliance reports?

1.   AWS Directory Service

2.   AWS Artifact

3.   Amazon Inspector

4.   AWS Trusted Advisor

Question 17

You are going to create snapshots from EBS volumes in another geographical location using the console. Where would you make the snapshots?

A. In another Availability Zone

B. In another data center

C. In another Edge location

D. In another Region

Question 18

What does S3 stand for?

A. Simple Storage Service

B. Simplified Storage Service

C. Simple Store Service

D. Service for Simple Storage

Question 19

Which statement is true regarding the AWS shared responsibility model?

A. The security of the IaaS services is the responsibility of AWS.

B. The security of managed services is the responsibility of the customer.

C. Duties vary depending on the services used.

D. Patching the guest O.S. is the responsibility of AWS for all services.

Question 20

Miller is working with a large data set, and he needs to import it into a relational database service. What AWS service will meet his needs?

A. RDS

B. DynamoDB

C. ElastiCache

D. Neptune

Question 21

What services/features are required to maintain a highly available and fault-tolerant architecture in AWS? (Choose two)

A. Elastic Load Balancer

B. CloudFormation

C. AWS NACL

D. Amazon EC2 Auto Scaling

Question 22

Which of the following aspects of security are managed by AWS? (Choose two)

A. Securing global physical infrastructure

B. Hardware patching

C. VPC security

D. Encryption of EBS volumes

E. Access permissions

Question 23

Which of the following AWS Support Plans gives you 24/7 access to Cloud Support Engineers via email & phone? (Choose two)

A. Premium

B. Developer

C. Business

D. Enterprise

E. Standard

Technology

AWS Organization and Accounts

Amazon Virtual Private Cloud (VPC)

After a region and AZ have been established, the customer will need a VPC. The VPC is where the customer will launch their AWS resources. It is their logically isolated portion of the cloud that gets assigned for their Use.

Internet Gateway

Next, the internet gateway will be enabled, which grants the customer access to the Internet and sets up the routing tables and network ACL (NACL). A subnet partitions a logical I.P. network into smaller portions or segments, like a housing development built on one property. Instead of one large house on 54 Main Street, there are now ten houses, and their addresses become a subdivision of the primary address.

Security Groups

A security group on AWS is a type of firewall positioned at the instance level of the cloud.

AWS Core Services

AWS comes with a host of core and integrated services to ensure customers get the services they need. These services can be broken into the following:

Database Services

There are several AWS database services, and some of the most widely used ones are:

AWS Relational Database Service (RDS)

RDS is the most commonly used of the database services on AWS because it supports multiple database engines. These database engines include:

- MySQL

- Maria DB

- Oracle

- Aurora

- Microsoft SQL

- Postgres

DymamoDB

It is a database that is based on Cassandra. It is a NoSQL key/value database. It will guarantee many reads or write per second.

ElastiCache

ElastiCache database is a caching source that is compatible with databases such as open-source Memcached and Redis.

Redshift

Redshift is a columnar store database that can run a warehouse-type application that requires petabytes of information. For all those that do not know, one petabyte (P.B.) is 1000 TB.

CloudFormation

It works for infrastructure as code and creates a template using either YAML or JSON file.

Elastic Beanstalk

It is a simple service used for scaling as well as deploying web applications. Elastic Beanstalk is compatible with applications created in .NET, PHP, Node.js, Python, Ruby, Docker, Java, and Go. It is a simple application for uploading code that needs little to no tweaking to work.

AWS Computing

AWS computing core services include the following:

Amazon Elastic Cloud Compute (EC2)

Amazon EC2 is a web service with the following features:

- Provides complete control

- Allows the configuration of capacity

- Provides resizable compute capacity

Everything on AWS runs on EC2 instances. It is an Elastic Compute cloud that allows for the operating system's full configuration, network, memory, and CPU in the cloud environment.

Elastic Container Service (ECS)

This service is highly scalable and provides Docker as a service. It offers high-performance orchestration of containers that supports Docker containers. The customer will have to pay for the EC2 to run this service.

Elastic Beanstalk

Elastic Beanstalk is the service that operates the various AWS services. These services include Simple Notification Services (SNS), EC2 Amazon S3, CloudWatch, Elastic Load Balancers, auto-scaling, and CloudWatch.

Lambda

Lambda is a service that you only pay for when it is in Use. It is a serverless service used to deploy or run code on without having to manage, invest in, or configure servers.

AWS Storage Services

Amazon Elastic Block Store (EBS)

Amazon EBS is used with Amazon EC2 instances to provide block-level storage volumes. EBS volumes exist independently from an example as they are off-instance storage volumes.

They are the virtual disk of the AWS cloud for which there are three types of EBS volumes:

- General Purpose (SSD)

- Magnetic

- Provisional IOPS (SSD)

Amazon Simple Storage Service (S3)

Amazon S3 is an internet or cloud storage space, much like DropBox or GoogleDrive. Only S3 can be used to store any size of data that can be accessed from anywhere over the web.

Amazon S3 features include:

- Object storage

- Can store any amount of data

- S3 is durable

- S3 is scalable

- Uses query in place

- S3 has flexible data management.

- Has flexible data transfer capabilities

- S3 is compatible and supported by AWS services as well as AWS partners, and various vendors.

Elastic File Storage (EFS)

This storage solution can be mounted to two or more EC2 instances at the same time.

Storage Gateway

Storage Gateway bridges the gap for Use with hybrid cloud solutions using local caching.

AWS Logging Services

AWS has a few services that help customers with system audit trails keep a close watch on changes to the AWS system and when those changes were made and by whom.

CloudTrail

CloudTrail audits and logs all calls that were made to APIs from AWS services. This service helps to determine pieces of information such as:

- AWS EC2 instance usage

- Who launched specific applications and when

- Who created a bucket

CloudTrail helps the customer to:

- Determine any misconfiguration that may have been made by a developer or administrator

- Create automated responses

- Help detect and deal with any malicious actors within the system

CloudWatch

CloudWatch comprises a host of different services used for logging information such as performance, various system metrics, and events. It is used to speed up delivery for customers of their content across the globe. Some of these services include:

- CloudWatch Alarms

- ○ Set threshold alarms, failure alarms, various alerts, etc.

- ○ Set notifications for various metrics

- ● CloudWatch Dashboard

- ○ A metrics-based dashboard that can be customized to visualize various logs, metrics, etc.

- ● CloudWatch Events

- ○ Service that will trigger an alarm for set thresholds

REVIEW QUESTIONS

Question 1

Under the AWS shared responsibility model, what are the customer's responsibilities? (Select TWO)

1: Physical and environmental security

2: Physical network devices including firewalls

3: Storage device decommissioning

4: Security of data in transit

5: Data integrity authentication

Question 2

A company plans to deploy a global commercial application on Amazon EC2 instances. The deployment solution is designed with the highest redundancy and fault tolerance.

Based on this situation, how should the EC2 instances be deployed?

1: In a single Availability Zone in one AWS Region

2: In a single Availability Zone in two AWS Regions

3: Across multiple Availability Zones in one AWS Region

4: In various Availability Zones in two AWS Regions

Question 3

Which benefit of the AWS Cloud eliminates the need for users to try estimating future infrastructure usage?

1: Easy global deployments

2: Security of the AWS Cloud

3: Elasticity of the AWS Cloud

4: Economies of scale

Question 4

Which AWS services can be used to connect the AWS Cloud and on-premises resources? (Select TWO)

1: AWS Managed VPN

2: Amazon Connect

3: Amazon CloudHSM

4: AWS Direct Connect

5: AWS Managed Services

Question 5

Where are Amazon EBS snapshots stored?

1: On an Amazon EBS instance store

2: On an Amazon EFS filesystem

3: Within the EBS block store

4: On Amazon S3

Question 6

A company has an application with users in both Australia and Germany. All the company infrastructure is currently provisioned in the Europe (Frankfurt) Region, and Australian users are experiencing high latency.

What should the company do to reduce latency?

1: Implement AWS Direct Connect for users in Australia

2: Provision resources in the Asia Pacific (Sydney) Region in Australia

3: Use AWS Transit Gateway to route users from Australia to the application quickly

4: Launch additional Amazon EC2 instances in Frankfurt to handle the demand

Question 7

Which AWS Support plan provides access to architectural and operational reviews, as well as 24/7 access to Cloud Support Engineers through email, online chat, and phone?

1: Basic

2: Business

3: Developer

4: Enterprise

Question 8

Which benefits can a company immediately realize using the AWS Cloud? (Select TWO)

1: Variable expenses are replaced with capital expenses

2: Capital expenses are replaced with variable expenses

3: User control of physical infrastructure

4: Increased agility

5: No responsibility for security

Question 9

Which service will enable you to run code as functions without needing to provision or manage servers?

1: Amazon EC2

2: AWS CodeDeploy

3: AWS Lambda

4: Amazon EKS

Question 10

An application that is deployed across multiple Availability Zones could be described as:

1: Being highly available

2: Having a global reach

3: Being secure

4: Having elasticity

Question 11

Which AWS tools can be used for automation? (Select TWO)

1: AWS Elastic Beanstalk

2: Elastic Load Balancing

3: AWS CloudFormation

4: Amazon Elastic File System (EFS)

5: AWS Lambda

Question 12

A user has an AWS account with a Business-level AWS Support plan and needs assistance with handling a production service disruption. Which action should the user take?

1: Contact the dedicated Technical Account Manager

2: Contact the dedicated AWS Concierge Support team

3: Open a business-critical system down support case

4: Open a production system down support case

Question 13

How does "elasticity" benefit an application design?

1: By reducing interdependencies between application components

2: By automatically scaling resources based on demand

3: By selecting the correct storage tier for your workload

4: By reserving capacity to reduce cost

Question 14

Which AWS storage technology can be considered a "virtual hard disk in the cloud"?

1: Amazon Elastic File Storage (EFS) filesystem

2: Amazon Elastic Block Storage (EBS) volume

3: Amazon S3 object

4: Amazon Glacier archive

Question 15

What is the scope of a VPC within a region?

1: Spans all Availability Zones within the region

2: Spans all Availability Zones globally

3: At least two subnets per region

4: At least 2 data centers per region

Question 16

A company needs protection from distributed denial of service (DDoS) attacks on its website and assistance from AWS experts during such events. Which AWS managed service will meet these requirements?

1: AWS Shield Advanced

2: AWS Firewall Manager

3: AWS Web Application Firewall

4: Amazon GuardDuty

Question 17

Which AWS security service provides a firewall at the subnet level within a VPC?

1: Security Group

2: IAM Policy

3: Bucket Policy

4: Network Access Control List

Question 18

Which AWS Cloud design principles can help increase reliability? (Select TWO)

1: Using monolithic architecture

2: Measuring overall efficiency

3: Testing recovery procedures

4: Adopting a consumption model

5: Automatically recovering from failure

Question 19

Which items can be configured from within the VPC management console? (Select TWO)

1: Subnets

2: Regions

3: Load Balancing

4: Auto Scaling

5: Security Groups

Question 20

Which of the following are accurate descriptions of AWS IAM users and groups? (Select TWO)

1: Groups can be nested and can contain other groups

2: A user can be a member of multiple groups

3: Groups can have users only and cannot be nested

4: A user can only be a member of a single group at one a time

5: All new users are automatically added to a default group

Question 21

What considerations are there when choosing which region to use? (Select TWO)

1: Data sovereignty

2: Available storage capacity

3: Latency

4: Pricing in local currency

5: Available compute capacity

Question 22

What technology enables calculate the ability to adjust as loads change?

1: Load balancing

2: Automatic failover

3: Round robin

4: Auto Scaling

Question 23

Based on the shared responsibility model, which of the following security and compliance tasks is AWS responsible for?

1: Granting access to individuals and services

2: Encrypting data in transit

3: Updating Amazon EC2 host firmware

4: Updating operating systems

Question 24

Which AWS technology can be referred to as a "virtual hard disk in the cloud"?

1: Amazon EFS Filesystem

2: Amazon S3 Bucket

3: Amazon EBS volume

4: Amazon ENI

Question 25

Which type of scaling does Amazon EC2 Auto Scaling provide?
1: Vertical

2: Linear

3: Horizontal

4: Incremental

Billing and Pricing

Reliability Design Principles

AWS advocates several design principles to enhance the reliability of your solution:

1. Testing recovery procedures

2. Automatically recover from failure

3. Scale horizontally to increase aggregate system availability.

4. Stop guessing capacity

5. Manage change in automation

Areas of Reliability

AWS partitions reliability into three areas:

1. Foundations

2. Change Management

3. Failure Management

AWS Reliability Foundations Services

The AWS reliability foundations services include:

1. AWS IAM

2. Amazon VPC

3. AWS Trusted Advisor

4.   AWS Shield

The AWS IAM, VPC, and Shield are covered elsewhere in this manuscript. Please refer to the table of contents.

AWS Trusted Advisor

At no charge, every AWS account has access to the AWS Trusted Advisor. Accessed from the AWS Management Console, the AWS Trusted Advisor helps AWS customers improve security and performance. Its prominent focus is on:

·   Service Limits

·   Security Groups

·   Specific Ports Unrestricted

·   IAM use

·   MFA on the AWS Root Account

·   Find under-utilized resources

The AWS Trusted Advisor provides customers with easy access to a variety of important performance and security recommendations. As reported by AWS, the most popular proposals involve:

·   Cost optimization

·   Security

·   Fault tolerance

·   Performance improvement; and

- Service checks

- The AWS Trusted Advisor is also a source of best practices that cover:

- Service limits;

- Security group rules that allow unrestricted access to specific ports ;

- IAM use;

- MFA on the root account;

- S3 bucket permissions;

- EBS public snapshots, and

- RDS available snapshots.

For AWS clients who have purchased the Business or Enterprise Support plans, there are additional checks and guidance available.

AWS Reliability Change Management Services

The AWS reliability change management services include:

- AWS CloudTrail

- AWS Config

- Amazon CloudWatch – this is the AWS service that is key to ensuring reliability.

- Auto Scaling

The above services are covered elsewhere in this manuscript. Please refer to the table of contents.

AWS Reliability Failure Management Services

The AWS reliability failure management services include:

· AWS CloudFormation

· Amazon S3

· Amazon Glacier

· AWS KMS

The above services are covered elsewhere in this manuscript. Please refer to the table of contents.

Reliability Design Patterns

In the AWS cloud, there are four common reliability design patterns:

1. Backup and Restore

2. Pilot Light Architecture

3. Fully Working Low-Capacity Standby Architecture

4. Multi-site Active-Active Architecture

Their preparation and disaster recovery phases will be explained for each design pattern. Then their RTO and RPO will be described.

Backup and Restore

The best that can be said of reliability based on backup and restore best practices is that the approach minimizes costs (i.e., you pay for storage of the backup images) and a simple solution that is easy to get started with.

Preparation Phase: Level 0 backup images of each system component have to be taken, and incremental backup photos are taken subsequently. These backup image files are stored in S3. To be able to restore the system' know-how' covering these matters are mandatory and must also be documented: which AMI to use/build, restoring from a backup image, configuring the deployment, smoothly switching over to the recovered components.

Disaster Recovery Phase: restore failed component(s) from their backup images, launch required infrastructure, switching over to the recovered/established parts.

RTO: this takes as long as it takes to restore from backup and then launch and switch over.

RPO: since the last time the backup image was made.

Pilot Light Architecture

A typical Pilot Light Architect has an on-premise system (the primary), which the DNS service (e.g., Amazon Route 53 points to). And in the AWS cloud, you have a secondary system that includes a replicate database that is a mirror image of the on-premise database. The other application components are also present in the cloud, but they are all minimally provisioned resources.

Preparation Phase: though the other application components are provisioned in the cloud, they are not running (other than the data replication processes). Of course, backups are being taken regularly, and recovery procedures must be fully documented and well known.

Disaster Recovery Phase: when the primary fails, the cloud components are automatically up-scaled and launched. The DNS service is then changed to point to the backup system now running in the AWS cloud.

RTO: the time it takes to detect the primary system failure and the automated provisioning of the AWS cloud's secondary system.

RPO: this depends on the frequency of data replication between the primary and the secondary.

Fully Working Low-Capacity Standby Architecture

In the fully working low-capacity standby architecture, there are two running systems, the fully provisioned primary and a low-capacity secondary, to which the DNS server is distributing requests. In this example, the low-capacity secondary is running in the AWS cloud.

Preparation Phase: the low-capacity secondary must be designed and built to auto-scale horizontally.

Disaster Recovery Phase: immediately begin to failover to the secondary, the low-capacity secondary is auto-scaled to match the capacity of the now-failed primary system, and the DNS server is changed to point only to the AWS cloud secondary system

RTO: as long as it takes the secondary to scale-up to primary capacity.

RPO: directly dependent on the type of data replication system being used.

Reliability Best Practices

AWS recommends the following reliability best practices:

1 Start simple and work towards more complex automation;

2 Be sure to take full backups of the AWS solutions;

3 Incrementally improve the RTO and RPO on an ongoing basis;

4 Exercise and practice disaster recovery procedures.

REVIEW QUESTIONS

Question 1

A company wants to monitor all events in their AWS account; in such a case, which of the following can help them out?

A. AWS S3

B. AWS CloudTrail

C. AWS TCO

D. AWS Trusted advisor

Question 2

Choose the options which correctly mention the responsibility of AWS according to the Shared Security Model? Choose threeanswers :

A. Securing edge locations

B. Managing Console

C. Monitoring physical device security

D. Implementing service organization Control (SOC) standards

Question 3

For non-stop Monitoring, logging, and auditing of physical access controls, which tool can be used?

A. Physical Security

B. User keyword

C. Local Guidance

D. Tertiary Security

Question 4

When public and private cloud services are mixed, the cloud formed will be?

A. Private Cloud

B. Public Cloud

C. Real Cloud

D. Hybrid Cloud

Question 5

A company wants to use an application where there is a significant amount of traffic. Which services can help them?

A. Single-purpose IOPS

B. General Purpose IOPS

C. Provisioned IOPS

D. Multipurpose IOPS

Question6

Can you suggest any other name for attributes?

A.   Series

B.   Indexes

C.   Fields

D.   Keys

Question 7

Select one of the vital features on Navigation Bar?

A. AWS S3

B. AWS Monitor Control

C. AWS Menu bar

D. AWS Region

Question 8

Direct Attached Storage is a kind of _____ Storage.

A. Amazon Elastic Block Storage

B. Read drive

C. Hard Disk Storage

D. Internal Storage

Question 9

A category recommendation that is not given by the AWS Trusted Advisor?

A. Groups

B. Low availability

C. Cost Optimization

D. Discipline

E. High Availability

Question 10

Let's suppose you have a Web application hosted in an EC2 Instance that needs to send notifications based on events. What service can you get help from?

A. AWS MFA

B. AWS SNS

C. AWS EC2

D. AWS EBS

Question 11

For transfer of a website to one type of cloud while its brochure is on another, which cloud can be used?

A. Real Cloud

B. Private Cloud

C. Dynamic Cloud

D. Hybrid Cloud

Question 12

Suppose you want to access the provided service in AWS, what do you prefer?

A.   AWS Security Groups

B.   AWS Hardware Development Kits

C.   AWS Software Development Kits

D.   AWS Enquiry API?s

Question 13

Your organization wants to use high-frequency processors, which instance type will you prefer?

A. Dedicated

B. M2

C. C3

D. On spot

Question 14

At the time of the disaster, what actions will you perform to safeguard your company?

A. Close your datacenter

B. Backup your mission static data

C. Scalable computing capacity routers

D. Launch the replacement compute capacity

Question 15

Choose any of the following two security requirements that are managed by AWS customers?

A. Physical security

B. Tertiary security

C. Password Policies

D. User permissions

E. Hardware patching

Question 16

When calculating Total Cost of Ownership (TCO) for the AWS Cloud, which factor must be considered?

A. The ability to choose the highest cost vendor

B. The number of users migrated out of AWS

C. The number of servers migrated to AWS

D. The number of users migrated to AWS

Question 17

A company wants access to all the checks in the Trusted Advisor Service, how can they do it? Choose two options.

A. Business

B. Enterprise

C. Account

D. Department

Question 18

XYZ company wants to use network services that would implement its code from Amazon EC2 instances on the virtual servers. What should the company use?

A. AWS console

B. Amazon E.C. dashboard

C. manual Scaling Service

D. AWS Lambda

Question 19

Choose the most appropriate option to use the DNS Web service?

A.   Amazon Route 53 Hosted Zones

B.   Manual Scaling Groups

C.   Hybrid cloud

D.   Private cloud

Question 20

Elastic Load Balancer has a higher fault-tolerance level. How?

A. Dividing instances into several Availability Zones

B. Launch the replacement compute capacity

C. Multiplying examples into one availability Zones

D. Destroying subnets

Question 21

Choose the option that is a scalable and economic amalgamation of your office I.T. and AWS storage infrastructure?

A. AWS MFA

B. AWS EBS Volume

C. Amazon CLI

D. AWS Storage Gateway

Question 22

What was the first service offered by Amazon to transfer data?

A. Disk

B. Snowball

C. AWS CLI

D. AWS POLICIES

Question 23

To examine the customer's AWS environment, identify security gaps, and fill them, which tool in AWS can be used?

A. Trusted Guide

B. Trusted Advisor

C. Trusted Counselor

D. Trusted Controller

Question 24

A part of the Enterprise support plan, which is the primary point of contact for the ongoing support needs?

A. TSM

B. SQL

C. SBS

D. TAM

Question 25

Which can be a fair use case for storing content in AWS RRS?

A. Storing large video files.

B. Keeping thumbnails & transcoded media

C. Storing a video file which is not producible

D. Storing frequently used log files.

AWS Services

The AWS administration that is fundamental to Reliability is Amazon CloudWatch, which screens runtime measurements. The associated administrations and highlights bolster the three regions in dependability:

· Foundations: AWS IAM empowers you to control access to AWS administrations, furthermore, assets safely. AWS Trusted Consultant gives perceivability into administration limits. AWS Shield is an overseen Distributed Forswearing of Service (DDoS) insurance administration that shields web applications are running on AWS.

· AWS Config gives a point by point stock of your AWS assets and setup, and persistently records design changes. Amazon AutoScaling is a help that will provide a computerized request to the executives for a conveyed outstanding task at hand. Amazon CloudWatch gives the capacity to alert on measurements, including custom measurements. Amazon CloudWatch likewise has logging include that it can utilize to total log records from your assets.

· Failure Management: AWS CloudFormation gives formats to the production of AWS assets and arrangements them in an organized and unsurprising manner. Amazon S3 offers profoundly sturdy assistance to keep reinforcements. Amazon Glacier gives exceptionally sturdy documents. AWS KMS provides a robust essential administration framework that incorporates numerous AWS administrations.

Execution Efficiency

The Performance Efficiency column incorporates the capacity to utilize processing assets productively to meet framework prerequisites and keep up that effectiveness as request changes and advances develop. You can discover prescriptive direction on Execution in the Execution Efficiency Pillar whitepaper.

The Standard for Execution:

There are five plan standards for execution proficiency in the cloud:

Democratize Cutting Edge Innovations:

Technologies that are hard to actualize can get simpler to devour by driving that information and multifaceted nature into the cloud seller's space. As opposed to having your I.T. group figure out how to have, what's more, run another innovation, they can permanently expend it as a help. For instance, NoSQL databases, media transcoding, and A.I. are generally advances that require the ability that isn't uniformly scattered over the specialized network. In the cloud, these innovations become administrations that your group can devour while concentrating on item improvement instead of asset provisioning.

Go worldwide in minutes:

Easily convey your framework in various regions around the world with only a couple of snaps. It permits you to give lower idleness and a superior experience for your clients at negligible expense.

Use serverless structures:

In the cloud, serverless designs evacuate the need to run and keep up servers to do conventional figure exercises. For model, stockpiling administrations can go about as static sites, expelling the requirement for web servers, and occasionally have your code for you. It does not just evacuate the operational weight of dealing with these servers. Yet, it can also bring down value-based costs because these oversaw administrations work at a cloud-scale. Test all the more regularly: With virtual and automatable assets, you can rapidly do comparative testing utilizing various kinds of cases, stockpiling, or setups.

Mechanical compassion:

Use the innovative approach that adjusts best to what you are attempting to achieve. For instance, consider information that gets to designs while choosing a database or capacity draws near.

Definition of execution proficiency in the cloud:

There are best practice zones for execution proficiency in the cloud:

· Selection

· Monitoring

· Trade-offs

Adopt an information-driven strategy in choosing elite engineering. Assemble information on all parts of the engineering, from the significant level structure to the determination, what's the more, design of asset types. By evaluating your decisions on a patterned premise, you will guarantee that you are exploiting the consistently advancing AWS Cloud. Checking will ensure that you know about any Cost Optimization.

Cost Optimization:

The Cost Optimization column incorporates the capacity to run frameworks to convey business esteem at the most reduced value point. The cost streamlining column gives a diagram of plan standards, best practices also, questions. You can discover prescriptive direction on usage in the Cost improvement Pillar whitepaper.

Plan Principles of Cost Improvement in the Cloud:

There are five structure standards for cost improvement in the cloud:

· Adopt a utilization model: Pay just for the figuring assets that you require and increment or diminishing use contingent upon business necessities, not by utilizing elaborate determining. For instance, improvement and test situations are commonly just used for eight hours per day during the workweek. You can stop these assets when they not used for a potential cost reserve funds of 75%

· Measure by and significant effectiveness: Measure the business yield of the remaining task at hand and the costs related to conveying it. Utilize this Measure to know the increases you make from expanding return and diminishing expenses.

· Stop burning through cash on server farm activities: AWS does the challenging work of racking, stacking, and controlling servers to concentrate on your clients and association extends as opposed to on I.T. foundation.

· Analyze and private consumption: The cloud makes it simpler to precisely distinguish the utilization and cost of frameworks, which at that point permits straightforward attribution of I.T. costs to singular remaining burden proprietors. These assist measures with returning on venture (ROI) and offer outstanding tasks at hand proprietors to upgrade their assets and diminish costs.

· Use oversaw and application-level administrations to decrease the cost of possession: In the cloud, managed and application-level administrations expel the operational weight of keeping up servers for errands, for example, sending an email or overseeing databases. As overseen administrations work at a cloud-scale, they can offer a lower cost for each exchange or, on the other hand, administration.

There are four best practice zones for cost improvement in the cloud:

· Consumption Awareness

· Cost-Effective Resources

· Matching market interest

· Optimizing Over Time

Similarly, as with different columns, there are trade-offs to consider. For instance, do you need to organize for speed to advertise or for cost? Now and again, it's ideal for organizing for speed—going to announce rapidly, transporting new highlights, or necessarily complying with a time constraint — as opposed to putting resources into direct cost streamlining. Plan choices are now and again guided by flurry rather than observational information, as the enticement consistently exists to overcompensate "in the event of some unforeseen issue" as opposed to investing energy benchmarking for the most cost-ideal remaining burden after some time. It frequently prompts over-provisioned what's more, under-upgraded arrangements, which stay static for a mind-blowing duration cycle. The associated segments give procedures and critical direction to the underlying and continuous cost enhancement of your method.

Consumption Awareness

The expanded adaptability and skill that the cloud empowers energizes advancement and quick-paced advancement and arrangement. It dispenses with the manual procedures and time-related with provisioning on-premises framework, including recognizing equipment particulars, arranging value citations, overseeing buy orders, planning shipments, and afterward conveying the assets. Be that as it may, the convenience what's more, for all intents and purposes boundless on-request limit, requires another perspective about consumptions.

Numerous organizations are made out of different frameworks run by other groups. The capacity to credit asset expenses to the individual association or item proprietors drives active utilization conduct and diminishes squander. Exact cost attribution permits you to know which items are productive and allows you to make more educated choices about where to assign spending plan.

In AWS, you can utilize Cost Explorer to follow your spending and increase bits of knowledge into precisely where you spend. Utilizing AWS Budgets, you can send warnings if your Use or, on the other hand, costs are not in line with your figures. You can utilize labeling on assets to apply business and association data to your utilization and value; this gives extra bits of knowledge to advancement from an association point of view.

Upgrading Over Time

As AWS discharges new administrations and highlights, it is a best practice to audit your current

structural choices to guarantee they keep on being the savviest. As your necessities change, be forceful in decommissioning assets, whole administrations, and frameworks that you do not require anymore. Overseen administrations from AWS can altogether enhance the remaining burden, so it is fundamental to know about new oversaw administrations and highlights as they become accessible. For a model, running an Amazon RDS database can be less expensive than running your Amazon EC2. The associated inquiries centeron these contemplations for cost advancement.

How to Secure Your AWS Resources

If you have created your account, the next step is securing your AWS resources. You need to follow some security best practices to safeguard your help in the cloud. After creating your account with a favorite e-mail and password in AWS's management console, you should always sign in your root account with these same credentials.

Avoid compromising your root account by adopting security best practices. The root account contains all resources and services in your account. Here are some tips to securing your account:

Creating a Strong Password for your Account in the Cloud

Use a strong password for your account. It involves a combination of numerals, memorable characters, and letters. It uses a third-party management tool for passwords designed to create and manage strong passwords.

Using a Group E-mail Alias

This feature enables other trusted members of your organization to access the account if you are unavoidably absent from responding to e-mails, notifications, and manage workloads in the cloud. You can also update your details in your account at any time.

Enable or Apply Multi-Factor Authentication Process

The multi-factor authentication process is a security feature providing an extra level of protection to your root account and your username and password. After signing in to your account with your user name and password, you should include an additional piece of information accessible to you alone. It is stored in a phone, app, or a reliable MFA hardware system.

Choose the type of multi-factor authentication device to use from the list of supported devices on the platform. If you are using a hardware system for storing your MFA, ensure the device is kept in a safe place. If your MFA is a virtual system such as software or phone, consider what happens to your passwords and e-mail addresses if the app is corrupted or missing.

The best method is to activate more than one device at once. You can also use a virtual system with options for password recovery.

Daily Account Access requires you to setup Groups, Users, and Roles.

If more than one person or various groups will be managing the system every day, create user groups and roles using the IAM (Identity and Access Management) resources. Activating this type of accessibility on the cloud will only grant permission to the IAM user group with specific roles that they are allowed to do in the system. It is also called the least privilege in Amazon Web Services.

Delete or Remove your Account's Access Keys

Using the command line together with Amazon APIs, you can allow programmatic access to your AWS resources. It is recommended that users should not create or use the access keys or passwords associated with their accounts for programmatic access into the cloud.

If you already have access keys, it is advisable to delete or remove them. However, create IAM users and grant such persons the necessary permissions they need to execute their workloads. It will enable you to issue access keys to your groups with the IAM user.

CloudTrail Should be Enabled

Enabling CloudTrail helps you in tracking every activity in your AWS resources. Turn on your cloud platform; this will assist the support center and your solutions engineer in devising possible security issues or configuration problems.

Identity and Accessibility Management in AWS

Now, you can enjoy secure accessibility and manage your AWS services and resources properly using AWS IAM – Identity and Access Management. With this, you can create and manage your user groups. It will enable you to use permissions to allow or deny access to unauthorized persons.

This feature is provided at no cost, but charges are incurred by using other AWS resources.

How Identity and Accessibility Management Works

a. Helps you manage the roles and permissions – IAM helps you create roles and manage their permissions in handling operations and services that could be performed by an entity or AWS service assuming the position. It enables you to define persons that can take specific roles in the platform. Another feature here is called service-linked functions that can help you to delegate permissions and roles to cloud resources on your behalf.

b. Handles Users and Accessibility – it is easy to create users and assign them personal security credentials such as passwords, access keys, and MFA. You can also demand temporary security credentials to provide users access to cloud resources and services. It is necessary to control permissions and regulate who can access the platform at any time.

c. Controls Federated Users and Permissions – identity federation for existing identities is a great feature for managing groups, users, and delegating roles. Apply other identity management solutions that support SAML 2.0, or you can use federation samples such as API federation or AWS Console SSO.

Best Practices for Identity and Accessibility Management in AWS

The best practices for IAM in AWS include:

· Turning on AWS CloudTrail for auditing.

· Enabling MFA for privileged users.

- Rotating security credentials regularly.

- Restricting exceptional accessibility further with conditions.

- Removing or reducing the Use of the root.

- Using IAM roles for sharing access to the platform.

- Applying IAM roles for Amazon EC2 instances.

- Configuring and maintaining a firm password policy.

- Creating individual users.

- Managing permissions with groups.

- Granting or offering the least privilege to users.

Use Cases for IAM in Amazon Web Services

1. Offers multi-factor authentication for privileged customers – high privileged users can access the cloud resources at no additional costs. It will provide them with the user name and password credentials. Moreover, users are requested to have a token for hardware MFA or use MFA-enabled mobile device with a valid MFA code.

2. Analyzing access across your AWS environment – with IAM in AWS, you can analyze access across your domain to enable your security administrators and teams to authenticate that your policies can provide the public and other users easy access to your online resources. These policies could be refined to give access to only the right services needed by users.

3. IAM integrates with your corporate directory – this feature grants your workers or users and applications federated access to the AWS service APIs and AWS management console. It is possible with existing identity systems like Microsoft's active directory. Other identity management solution supporting SAML 2.0 or federation samples such as API federation.

4. Provides Smooth access to AWS resources – this feature gives you unrestricted access to AWS service APIs, including specific cloud resources. It enables you to add the time of day that someone can access the platform, including their original I.P. addresses. This case will indicate if the users have SSL or they have authenticated an MFA device.

Authentication Processes

The authentication process of your Identity and Accessibility Management is done using a multi-factor authentication process. It is an easy best practice that adds a layer of protection to your user name and password in the cloud.

It involves a two-step process for verifying your accessibility to the cloud platform.

a. If you sign in to the AWS management console, you will be prompted to enter your user name and password. That is the first factor, which is based on what you know.

b. The second factor is that you will be requested to put in an authentication code for your Amazon Web Service MFA device.

Both of these authentication processes provide a reliable security feature for your AWS resources and account settings. This authentication process could be enabled for your personal IAM users created under your account name. The multi-factor authentication process could be used for controlling accessibility to service APIs in Amazon Web Services. No charges will be made on your AWS account after setting up a supported hardware device or virtual multi-factor authentication device. Cross-account accessibility to the cloud platform can be protected using MFA procedures.

The Roles of User Groups in AWS

User groups could be assigned an existing IAM role in the directory of Amazon Web Services. There should be a reliable relationship with the AWS directory service.

Here are the processes to assign groups of users to existing IAM user groups in AWS.

· Scroll to the navigation pane of Amazon Web Services (AWS) directory service console and click on Directories.

· On the drop-down menu on the Directories page, select your directory I.D.

· Go to the directory details menu and click on the Application management button.

· Scroll to the AWS Management console menu and click on Delegate console access. Select the IAM role name for an existing IAM role, which you want to assign to other users. If you notice that the function has not yet been created, see Creating a New Role.

· Click on the selected or designated role menu page. Go to Manage Users and groups for this role and click the Add button.

· Go to the Add groups or users to the role menu page and click on choose active directory Forest

Select the on-premises forest, a trusted forest, or Amazon Web Services managed Microsoft A.D. forest, referred to as this forest. Either of these forests is designed for accessing the AWS management console.

· Locate and click on Specify which groups or users to add. Choose either Find by Group or Find by User. Enter the name of the group or user in the box provided. Use the list on the menu page to add for possible matches with your desired group.

· Click on Add and finish assigning the groups and users to the role.

Access for users in nested groups in your directory is not supported. Members or users of the parent group have access to the console, while children groups don't have such access.

Conclusion

Amazon continues to roll out new regional places, so you're most likely to have access to a neighboring service location and the abundant AWS ecosystem.

AWS Is the Leading Cloud-Computing Provider. AWS is exceptionally popular. However, its popularity has the impact of making the service much better. Today, Amazon has an enhancing cycle taking place:

- Having more users produces a higher volume of usage, which increases the amount of hardware Amazon purchases, which reduces its costs utilizing economies of scale, which are handed down to users in the type of lower prices.

-Because of the large number of users, companies that use complimentary services (online application integration, for example) decide to initially put their services in AWS, which makes the total service much better, which draws in more users.

-As more people and companies use AWS, more understanding is made available in human capital and other resources (like this book!).

This knowledge makes it easier for new users to start and be productive quickly, making AWS more attractive.

AWS's popularity and acknowledge that its status as the most prominent cloud provider brings considerable advantages to you and that, moreover, those benefits will continue to grow as the service. It's another present that keeps providing.

AWS Enables Innovation.

Everywhere you turn, the word development is a hot subject. Individuals acknowledge that innovation makes life much better and can improve the future for generations to come. All of the incumbent innovation market leaders had no reward for altering the method they did the company.

AWS has changed how technology is provided to clients and, as a result, has enabled a surge of development. The development and low cost related to AWS permit little and big business to rapidly and cheaply introduce brand-new offerings as one development consultant put it:

AWS has decreased the cost of failure. AWS lets you quickly check out a brand-new item to see whether it "gets traction. On the other hand, if the service does not attain adoption, that's no issue-- the ease of shutting down. AWS resources mean that very little is lost if an ingenious perspective offering does not turn out.".meanorecast that a lot more innovation will happen as more individuals and companies become knowledgeable about AWS and its capabilities. AWS will be to the details.

AWS Is Cost Effective.

Much of that expense reduction is because of AWS: its on-demand low prices and simple termination without any charges make it possible to utilize and spend precisely as much computing capacity as you require when you require it.

The expense effectiveness of AWS isn't limited to start-ups, though. Every company can take advantage of access to inexpensive computing that doesn't need a prolonged commitment. It's a sign of the significantbenefits of AWS that much.

When there, the existing supplier community is terrified of what will occur.

Customers begin to demand AWS-like prices and benefit from them.

Amazon is a different company. Unlike many companies that strive for effectiveness to raise their own earnings margins, Amazon passes on the advantages of energy at lower costs. There's no factor to anticipate that this method will change.

It's substantially more expense significant than the conventional mode of acquiring.

By far, the leading cloud computing supplier in the industry, Amazon Web Services, is growing at rates of more than 100 percent. Its record of innovation and rate competitiveness is unrivaled in the market. I forecast that ten years from now, AWS will be the Microsoft or Google of its period. Your organization should become knowledgeable about AWS and determine how to utilize it successfully-- otherwise, it may discover itself the IT equivalent of a buggy whip maker after Henry Ford developed the assembly line.

AWS Is Good for Your Career.

Great careers are constructed on being the best individual in the best location at the right time. Being the best individual is all about you-- your capability for effort, Productive work relationships, and intelligence.

These attributes will assist you to succeed no matter which field or function you operate in.

However, remaining in the ideal place at the perfect time has a lot to do with insight about where a brand-new market, made possible by some development, is emerging and planting your flag there. In the 1920s or into the tv service in the 1950s or the Internet in the 1990s, people who moved into the vehicle industry experienced enormous opportunities as a new market searched for expertise to enable terrific companies to be built.

Technology innovation produces powerful abilities gaps in the market and makes those with understanding and experience necessary. Suppose you think that AWS is. The next-generation platform, too, can represent "the best place at the time" for you.

Answers to Review Questions

Cloud Concepts

Question1 Answer(s): 3, 4

Explanation:

Subnets and Security groups can be configured from within the VPC console.

CORRECT: "Subnets" is the right answer.

CORRECT: "Security Groups" is the right answer.

INCORRECT: "Regions" is incorrect. Regions are not configured, resources within regions are configured.

INCORRECT: "Load Balancing" is incorrect. Load balancing is configured from the EC2 console.

INCORRECT: "Auto Scaling" is incorrect. Auto scaling is configured from the EC2 console.

Question 2 Answer: 4

Explanation:

Elasticity means that your infrastructure scales are based on actual usage. When you have higher demand, you use more infrastructure and pay more, and when you have less demand, you need less infrastructure and pay less. The benefits are you don't need to guess about capacity and pay only for what you need.

CORRECT: "Elasticity of the AWS Cloud" is the right answer.

INCORRECT: "Easy global deployments" is incorrect. It is easy to deploy many AWS resources globally. Still,thisbenefit does not eliminate the need to estimate future usage.

INCORRECT: "Security of the AWS Cloud" is incorrect. The security of the AWS Cloud is important but does not eliminate the need to estimate future usage.

INCORRECT: "Economies of scale" is incorrect. This means you pay less for some resources because of the benefits of AWS's scale. However, this benefit does not eliminate the need to estimate future usage.

Question 3 Answer: 4

Explanation:

Only the Enterprise plan provides a response time of < 15 minutes for the failure of a business-critical system.

Both Business and Enterprise offer < 1-hour response time for the failure of a production system.

CORRECT: "Enterprise" is the right answer.

INCORRECT: "Business" is incorrect as described above.

INCORRECT: "Basic" is incorrect as described above.

INCORRECT: "Developer" is incorrect as described above.

Question 4 Answer(s):3, 5

Explanation:

Shared Controls– Controls which apply to both the infrastructure layer and customer layers, but in completely separate contexts or perspectives

Patch Management– AWS is responsible for patching and fixing flaws within the infrastructure, but customers are responsible for patching their guest OS and applications

Configuration Management– AWS maintains the configuration of itsinfrastructuredevices. Still, a customer is responsible for configuring their own guest operating systems, databases, and applications.

CORRECT: "Patch management" is a right answer.

CORRECT: "Configuration management" is also theright answer.

INCORRECT: "Storage system patching" is incorrect. Storage system patching is an AWS responsibility.

INCORRECT: "Physical and environmental" is incorrect. Physical and Environmental controls is an example of an inherited power (a customer fully inherits from AWS).

INCORRECT: "Service and Communications Protection" is incorrect. Service and Communications Protection is an example of a customer specific control.

Question 5 Answer: 1

Explanation:

Elasticity allows you to deploy your application without worrying about whether it will need more or fewer resources in the future. With elasticity, the infrastructure can scale on-demand, and you only pay for what you use.

CORRECT: "Elasticity" is the right answer.

Question 6Answer: 2, 4

Explanation:

Amazon S3 uses a universal (global) namespace, which means bucket names must be unique globally. However, you create the buckets in a region, and the data never leaves that region unless explicitly configured to do so through cross-region replication (CRR).

CORRECT: "Bucket names must be unique globally," is theright answer.

CORRECT: "Buckets are region-specific" is also a right answer.

INCORRECT: "Bucket names must be unique regionally" is incorrect as they must be globally unique.

INCORRECT: "Buckets are replicated globally," is incorrect. Objects within a bucket are replicated within a region across multiple AZs (except for the One-Zone IA class).

INCORRECT: "Buckets can contain other buckets" is incorrect. You cannot create nested buckets.

Question 7 Answer: 4, 5

Explanation:

The AWS Global infrastructure is built around Regions and Availability Zones (AZs). A Region is a physical location in the world where AWS has multiple AZs. AZs consist of one or more discrete data centers, each with redundant power, networking, and connectivity, housed in separate facilities

CORRECT: "Regions" is a right answer.

CORRECT: "Availability Zones" is also a right answer.

INCORRECT: "Clusters" is incorrect as this is not part of the AWS global infrastructure.

INCORRECT: "Fault Zones" is incorrect as this is not part of the AWS global infrastructure.

INCORRECT: "IP subnets" is incorrect as this is not part of the AWS global infrastructure.

Question 8 Answer: 2

Explanation:

S3 One Zone-IA is for data that is accessed less frequently, but requires rapid access when needed. Unlike other S3 Storage Classes which store data in a minimum of three Availability Zones (AZs), S3 One Zone-IA stores data in a single AZ and costs 20% less than S3 Standard-IA.

It's a good choice for storing secondary backup copies of on-premises data or easily re-creatable data. You can also use it as cost-effective storage for data that is replicated from another AWS Region using S3 Cross-Region Replication.

CORRECT: "Amazon S3 One Zone-Infrequent Access" is the right answer.

INCORRECT: "Amazon S3 Standard" is incorrect as this is a more resilient storage class and will cost more, so it not optimized for these requirements.

INCORRECT: "Amazon S3 Glacier Deep Archive" is incorrect. This storage class is suited to archival and takes several hours to restore data.

INCORRECT: "Amazon S3 Glacier" is incorrect. This storage class is suited to archival and takes minutes to hours to restore data.

Question 9 Answer: 2

Explanation:

Bootstrapping is the execution of automated actions to services such as EC2 and RDS. This is typically in the form of scripts that run when the instances are launched.

CORRECT: "Bootstrapping" is the right answer.

INCORRECT: "Golden Images" is incorrect. Golden Images are snapshots of pre-configured EBS volumes that can be used to launch new instances. You do this using Amazon Machine Images (AMIs).

INCORRECT: "Containerization" is incorrect. Containers are packaged software that runs in a Docker image. Services such as Amazon ECS and Fargate can run Docker containers.

INCORRECT: "Workflow automation" is incorrect. Workflow automation is a process or orchestrating automated actions—this is associated with services such as Chef and Puppet or AWS OpsWorks.

Question 10 Answer: 4

Explanation:

Amazon Simple Notification Service (Amazon SNS) is a web service that makes it easy to set up, operate, and send notifications from the cloud. Amazon SNS is used for building and integrating loosely-coupled, distributed applications.

NOTE: Sometimes AWS will expand abbreviations in answers and other times, like with this question, you just get the abbreviation. Therefore, there's no workaround; you have to know your abbreviations!

CORRECT: "Amazon SNS" is the right answer.

INCORRECT: "Amazon EBS" is incorrect. Amazon Elastic Block Storage (EBS) provides storage volumes for EC2 instances.

INCORRECT: "Amazon EFS" is incorrect. Amazon Elastic File System (EFS) provides an NFS filesystem for usage by EC2 instances.

INCORRECT: "Amazon RDS" is incorrect. Amazon Relational Database Service (RDS) provides a managed relational database service.

Question 11 Answer: 2

Explanation:

EFS is a fully-managed service that makes it easy to set up and scale file storage in the Amazon Cloud. EFS filesystems are mounted using the NFS protocol (which is a file-level protocol).

Access to EFS file systems from on-premises servers can be enabled viaDirect Connect or AWS VPN.

You mount an EFS file system on your on-premises Linux server using the standard Linux mount command for mounting a file system via the NFSv4.1 or NFSv5 protocol.

CORRECT: "Amazon EFS" is the right answer.

INCORRECT: "Amazon S3" is incorrect. Amazon S3 is an object-level, not a file-level storage system.

INCORRECT: "Amazon EBS" is incorrect. Amazon Elastic Block Storage (EBS) is block-level storage that can only be accessed by EC2 instances from the same AZ as the EBS volume.

INCORRECT: "Amazon Glacier" is incorrect. Amazon Glacier is an archiving solution that is accessed through S3.

Question 12 Answer: 1

Explanation:

AWS Lambda is a serverless compute service that runs your code in response to events and automatically manages the underlying compute resources for you.

Lambda runs your code on high-availability compute infrastructure and performs all the administration of the total resources, including server

98

and operating system maintenance, capacity provisioning and automatic scaling, code and security patch deployment, and code monitoring and logging. All you need to do is supply the code.

CORRECT: "AWS Lambda" is the right answer.

INCORRECT: "Amazon EC2" is incorrect. With Amazon EC2, you must manage the instance and operating system.

INCORRECT: "AWS CodeDeploy" isincorrect. AWS CodeDeployis a fully managed deployment service that automates software deployments to a variety of computing services such as Amazon EC2, AWS Lambda, and your on-premises servers.

INCORRECT: "Amazon EKS" is incorrect. Amazon ElasticContainerService for Kubernetes (Amazon EKS) is a managed service that makes it easy for you to run Kubernetes on AWS withoutneeding to stand up or maintain your own Kubernetes control plane

Question 13 Answer: D

OFFICIAL EXPLANATION:

Through a hybrid cloud, a company can retain control over an internally managed private cloud, while depending on the public cloud, when required. For example, during peak time, you can migrate a few applications to the public cloud. In cloud computing, the hybrid cloud refers to the use of both on-premises resources in addition to public cloud resources.

Question 14 Answer: D

OFFICIAL EXPLANATION:

Through a hybrid cloud, a company can retain control over an internally managed private cloud, while depending on the public cloud, when required. For example, during peak time, you can migrate a few applications to the public cloud. In cloud computing, the hybrid cloud refers to the use of both on-premises resources in addition to public cloud resources.

Question 15 Answer: A, C

OFFICIAL EXPLANATION:

Physical infrastructure is the responsibility of AWS and not with the customer. Hence it is not an advantage of moving to the AWS Cloud, And AWS provides security mechanisms. Still, even the responsibility of security lies with the customer.

Question 16 Answer: 4, 5

Explanation:

With infrastructure as code AWS assets are programmable, so you can apply techniques, practices, and tools from software development to make your whole infrastructure reusable, maintainable, extensible, and testable.

With bootstrapping, you can execute automated actions to modify default configurations. This includes scripts that install software or copy data to bring that resource to a particular state.

CORRECT: "Bootstrapping" is a right answer.

CORRECT: "Infrastructure as code" is also theright answer.

INCORRECT: "Snapshotting" is incorrect. Snapshotting is about saving data, not instantiating resources.

INCORRECT: "Fault tolerance" is incorrect. Fault tolerance is a method of increasing the availability of your system when components fail.

INCORRECT: "Performance monitoring" is incorrect. Performance monitoring has nothing to do with instantiating resources.

Question 17 Answer: 4

Explanation:

AWS allows customers to assign metadata to their AWS resources,in the form of tags. Each tag is a simple label consisting of a customer-defined key and an optional value that can make it easier to manage, search for, and filter resources. AWS Cost Explorer and detailed billing reports support the ability to break down AWS costs by tag.

The other options are incorrect as they are not methods of adding metadata to an AWS resource.

CORRECT: "Tagging" is the right answer.

INCORRECT: "Labelling" is incorrect as explained above.

INCORRECT: "Access Control" is incorrect as explained above.

INCORRECT: "Categorizing" is incorrect as explained above.

Question 18 Answer: 1

Explanation:

An Amazon Virtual Private Cloud (VPC) spans all availability zones within a region.

CORRECT: "Spans all Availability Zones within the region" is the right answer.

INCORRECT: "Spans all Availability Zones globally," is incorrect. VPCs do not span regions; you create VPCs in each region.

INCORRECT: "At least two subnets per region" is incorrect. VPCs are not limited by subnets, subnets are created within AZs, and you can have many subnets in an AZ

INCORRECT: "At least 2 data centers per region" is incorrect.

Question 19 Answer: 4

Explanation:

AWS CodeCommitis a fully-managed source control service that hosts secure Git-based repositories. It makes it easy for teams to collaborate on code in a secure and highly scalable ecosystem.

CORRECT: "AWS CodeCommit" is the right answer.

INCORRECT: "AWS CodeStar" isincorrect. AWS CodeStar enables you to develop, build, and deploy applications on AWS quickly. AWS CodeStarprovides a unified user interface, enabling you to easily manage your software development activities in one place.

INCORRECT: "AWS Cloud9" is incorrect. AWS Cloud9 is a cloud-based integrated development environment (IDE) that lets you write, run, and debug your code with just a browser.

INCORRECT: "AWS CodeDeploy" isincorrect. AWS CodeDeployis a deployment service that automates application deployments to Amazon EC2 instances, on-premisesinstances, or serverless Lambda functions.

Question 20 Answer: 4, 5

Explanation:

Elastic Web-Scale computing– you can increase or decrease capacity within minutes not hours and commission one to thousands of instances simultaneously.

Inexpensive – Amazon passes on the financial benefits of scale by chargingmeager rates and on a capacity consumed basis.

CORRECT: "Elastic web-scale computing" is a right answer.

CORRECT: "Inexpensive" is also theright answer.

INCORRECT: "High-availability with an SLA of 99.999%" is incorrect. AWS provide an SLA for EC2 that states that services will be available within each AWS region with a Monthly Uptime Percentage of at least 99.99%

INCORRECT: "Complete control of the hypervisor layer" is incorrect. Amazon EC2 does not provide any control of the hypervisor or underlying hardware infrastructure.

Question 21 Answer: 1

Explanation:

Amazon EC2 Auto Scaling automatically responds to demand by adding or removing EC2 instances to ensure the right amount of computing capacity is available at any time. This can help to automatically adjust the number of instances based on the load on your application.

CORRECT: "Amazon EC2 Auto Scaling" is the right answer.

INCORRECT: "AWS ElastiCache" is incorrect. AWS ElastiCacheprovidesin-memory cache and database services

INCORRECT: "Amazon Elastic Load Balancing" is incorrect. Amazon ELB distributes incoming requests to EC2 instances. It can be used in conjunction with Auto Scaling

INCORRECT: "Amazon DynamoDB" isincorrect. DynamoDB is a non-relational (NoSQL)

Question 22 Answer: 3

Explanation:

As application complexity increases, a desirable attribute of an IT system is that it can be broken into smaller, loosely coupled components. This means that IT systems should be designed in a way that reduces interdependencies—a change or a failure in one part should not cascade to other components

The concept of loose coupling includes "well-defined interfaces," which reduce interdependencies in a system by enabling interaction only through specific, technology-agnostic interfaces (e.g., RESTful APIs).

CORRECT: "Loose Coupling," is the right answer.

INCORRECT: "Services, Not Servers" is incorrect. This best practice encourages the use of a wider variety of AWS services in your application architectures.

INCORRECT: "Removing Single Points of Failure" is incorrect. This best practice aims to increase system availability.

INCORRECT: "Automation" is incorrect. This best practice encourages the use of automation for efficiency and consistency.

Question 23 Answer: 1

Explanation:

AWS CloudFormationprovides a common language for you to describe and provision all the infrastructure resources in your cloud environment.

CloudFormation allows you to use a simple text file to model and provision, in an automated and secure manner, all the resources needed for your applications across all regions and accounts.

CORRECT: "AWS CloudFormation" is the right answer.

INCORRECT: "AWS Elastic Beanstalk" is incorrect. AWS Elastic Beanstalk is used for running applications in a managed environment. It is not used for deploying templated configurations.

INCORRECT: "AWS CodeBuild" isincorrect. AWS CodeBuildis a fully managed continuous integration service that compiles source code runs tests, and produces software packages that are ready to deploy.

INCORRECT: "AWS CodeDeploy" isincorrect. AWS CodeDeployis a fully managed deployment service that automates software deployments to a variety of computingservices such as Amazon EC2, AWS Lambda, and on-premises servers. It does not use a templated configuration for deployment.

Question 24 Answer: 4

Explanation:

Latency (slow response times) is experienced when resources are far away. Distance is the single biggest factor that causes latency. The easiest option presented to resolve this situation is to place resources closer to where the users are.

CORRECT: "Provision resources in the Asia Pacific (Sydney) Region in Australia" is the correct answer.

INCORRECT: "Implement AWS Direct Connect for users in Australia" is incorrect. Direct Connect is a private network connection from your network or data centerinto a nearby AWS Region. This does not solve the latency issues.

INCORRECT: "Use AWS Transit Gateway to quickly route users from Australia to the application" is incorrect. This service is used to connect Amazon Virtual Private Clouds (VPCs) and on-premises networks to a single gateway for connecting multiple VPCs and on-premises networks. This does not solve the latency issues.

INCORRECT: "Launch additional Amazon EC2 instances in Frankfurt to handle the demand" is incorrect. Latency will still be an issue even with more resources in Frankfurt.

Question 25Correct Answer(s): 1

Explanation:

As application complexity increases, a desirable attribute of an IT system is that it can be broken into smaller, loosely coupled components.

This means that IT systems should be designed in a way that reduces interdependencies—a change or a failure in one component should not cascade to other parts.

CORRECT: "Implement loose coupling" is the right answer.

Security

Question 1 Correct Answer(s): 3, 4

Explanation:

Under the AWS shared responsibility model, AWS are responsible for security "of" the cloud and customers are responsible for security "in" the cloud. Securing data in transit and ensuring the integrity of data are customer responsibilities. Customers are always responsible for managing data including encryption.

CORRECT: "Security of data in transit" is a right answer.

CORRECT: "Data integrity authentication" is also a right answer.

Question 2 Correct Answer(s): B, E

Explanation:

"Inherited Controls are controls which a customer fully inherits from AWS such as physical controls and environmental controls.

For example: Let's say you have built an application in AWS for customers to store their data securely. But your customers are concerned about the security of the data and ensuring compliance requirements are met. To address this, you assure your customer that "our company does not host customer data in its corporate or remote offices, but rather in AWS data centers that have been certified to meet industry security standards."That includes physical and environmental controls to secure the data, which is the responsibility of Amazon. Companies do not have physical access to the AWS data centers. As such, they fully inherit the biological and environmental controls from AWS.

You can read more about AWS' data center controls here:

https://aws.amazon.com/compliance/data-center/controls/

Option A is not correct. Communications controls are the responsibility of the customer.

Options C & D are not correct. Patch Management and Configuration Management have shared controls.

Question 3 Correct Answer(s): 3

Explanation:

Identity and access management (IAM) Policies are documents that define permissions and can be applied to users, groups, and roles. IAM policies can be written to grant access to Amazon S3 buckets.

CORRECT: "IAM Policy" is the right answer.

Question 4 Correct Answer(s): 1, 3

Explanation:

AWS is responsible for the "security of the cloud." This includes protecting the infrastructure that runs all of the services offered in the AWS Cloud. This infrastructure is composed of the hardware, software, networking, and facilities that run AWS Cloud services.

The customer is responsible for "security in the cloud." Customer responsibility depends on the service consumed but includes aspects such as Identity and Access Management (includes password policies), encryption of data, protection of network traffic, and operating system, network and firewall configuration.

Question 5 Correct Answer(s): 3

Explanation:

The identity and access management service (IAM) is used to control individual and group access to AWS resources securely. IAM can also be used to manage multi-factor authentication (MFA). With MFA, you add an additional factor of authentication such as Google Authenticator device. This is "something you have" and is used with your password "something, you know."

CORRECT: "AWS IAM" is the right answer.

Question 6 Correct Answer(s): 3, 4

Explanation:

AWS is responsible for "Security of the Cloud" and customers are responsible for "Security in the Cloud."

AWS is responsible for items such as the physical security of the DC, replacement of old disk drives, and patch management of the infrastructure

Customers are responsible for items such as configuring security groups, network ACLs, patching their operating systems and encrypting their data

CORRECT: "Configuration of security groups" is a right answer.

CORRECT: "Encryption of customer data," is also theright answer.

Question 7 Correct Answer(s): 2, 3

Explanation:

AWS Key Management Service (KMS) gives you centralized control over the encryption keys used to protect your data. AWS CloudHSMis a cloud-based hardware security module (HSM) that enables you to easily generate and use your encryption keys on the AWS Cloud.

CORRECT: "AWS CloudHSM" is a right answer.

CORRECT: "AWS KMS" is also theright answer.

Question 8 Correct Answer(s): 2, 3

Explanation:

For extra security, AWS recommends that you require multi-factor authentication (MFA) for all users in your account. With MFA, users, have a device that generates a response to an authentication challenge.

Both the user's credentials (something you know) and the device-generated response (something you have) are required to complete the sign-in process. If a user's password or access keys are compromised, your account resources are still secure because of the additional authentication requirement.

Additionally, strong password policies should be used to enforce measures including minimum password length, complexity, and password reuse restrictions.

CORRECT: "AWS Multi-Factor Authentication (AWS MFA)" is a right answer.

CORRECT: "Strong password policies" is also theright answer.

Question 9 Correct Answer(s): 3

Explanation:

Inspector is an automated security assessment service that helps improve the security and compliance of applications deployed on AWS. The Inspector automatically assesses applications for vulnerabilities or deviations from best practices.

CORRECT: "Use AWS Inspector" is the right answer.

Question 10 Correct Answer(s): 3

Explanation:

AWS Key Management Service gives you centralized control over the encryption keys used to protect your data. You can create, import, rotate, disable, delete, define usage policies for, and audit the use of encryption keys used to encrypt your data.

Note: Make sure you know your abbreviations! Sometimes AWS will expand them and other times they won't, it varies by question. Therefore, you must know the abbreviations for all services in scope for the exam.

CORRECT: "AWS KMS" is the right answer.

Question 11 Correct Answer(s): 4

Explanation:

AWS WAF is a web application firewall that protects against common exploits that could compromise application availability, compromise security or consume excessive resources.

CORRECT: "AWS WAF" is the right answer.

Question 12 Correct Answer(s): 1

Explanation:

Groups are collections of users and have policies attached to them. You can use groups to assign permissions to multiple users. To do this, place the users in the group and then create an IAM policy with the correct permissions and attach it to the group.

You do not use an IAM User, Role, or password policy to assign permissions to multiple users.

CORRECT: "IAM Group" is the right answer.

Question 13 Correct Answer(s): 3

Explanation:

With IAM Roles, you can delegate permissions to resources for users and services without using permanent credentials (e.g., username and password). To do so, you can create a role and assign an IAM policy to the part that has the permissions required.

CORRECT: "IAM Role" is the right answer.

Question 14 Correct Answer(s): 2

Explanation:

You cannot associate an access key ID and secret access key with an IAM Group, Role, or Policy.

CORRECT: "IAM User" is the right answer.

Question 15 Correct Answer(s): 3

Explanation:

AWS Config is a fully-managed service that provides you with an AWS resource inventory, configuration history, and configuration change notifications to enable security and regulatory compliance.

CORRECT: "Configure AWS Configwith the resource types" is the right answer.

Question 16 Correct Answer(s): 2

Explanation:

AWS Artifactis the go-to, central resource for compliance-related information that matters to you. It provides on-demand access to AWS' security and compliance reports and select online agreements.

Reports availablein AWS ArtifactincludeServiceOrganization Control (SOC) reports, Payment Card Industry (PCI) reports, and certifications from accreditation bodies across geographies and compliance verticals that validate the implementation and operating effectiveness of AWS security controls.

CORRECT: "AWS Artifact" is the right answer.

Question 17 Answer: D

Explanation:

"Since you are going to create snapshots in another geographical location, then you will make them in another AWS Region.

Question 18 Answer: A

Explanation:

"Amazon Simple Storage Service (Amazon S3) is AWS' large, secure, and feature-rich object storage service

Question 19 Answer: C

Explanation:

"Customers should be aware that their responsibilities may vary depending on the AWS services chosen. For example, when using Amazon EC2, you are responsible for applying the operating system and application security patches regularly. However, such patches are applied automatically when using Amazon RDS.

Question 20 Answer: A

Explanation:

"RDS is the AWS's relational database service.

Question 21 Answer: A, D

Explanation:

"** Amazon EC2 Auto Scaling continually monitors the utilization of the instances underlying your application to make sure that your application always has the right amount of computing. In other words, Amazon EC2 Auto Scaling automatically scales the models up during demand spikes (to increase the availability of the application) or scales them down when demand lulls (to minimize costs).

Question 22 Answer: A, B

Explanation:

"AWS is continuously innovating the design and systems of its data centers to protect them from human-made and natural risks. For example, at the first layer of security, AWS provides several security features depending on the location, such as security guards, fencing,

115

security feeds, intrusion detection technology, and other security measures.

According to the Shared Responsibility Model, Patching of the underlying hardware is the AWS's responsibility. AWS is responsible for patching and fixing flaws within the infrastructure. Still, customers are responsible for repairing their guest OS and applications.

Question 23 Answer: 1, 5

Explanation:

Both AWS KMS and AWS CloudHSM can be used to generate data encryption keys. You use what is called customer master keys (CMKs) to create data encryption keys. The data encryption keys can then be used actually to encrypt the data.

CORRECT: "AWS Key Management Service (AWS KMS)" is a right answer.

CORRECT: "AWS CIoudHSM" is also theright answer.

INCORRECT: "Amazon Macie" isincorrect. Amazon Macieis a fully managed data security and data privacy service that uses machine learning and pattern matching to discover and protect your sensitive data in AWS

INCORRECT: "AWS Certificate Manager" is incorrect. AWS Certificate Manager is a service that lets you easily provision, manage, and deploy public and private Secure Sockets Layer/Transport Layer Security (SSL/TLS) certificates for use with AWS services and your internal connected resources.

Technology

Question 1 Answer: 4, 5

Explanation:

Under the AWS shared responsibility model, AWS is responsible for security "of" the cloud, and customers are responsible for security "in" the cloud. Securing data in transit and ensuring the integrity of data are customer responsibilities. Customers are always responsible for managing data, including encryption.

CORRECT: "Security of data in transit" is theright answer.

CORRECT: "Data integrity authentication" is also theright answer.

INCORRECT: "Physical and environmental security" is wrong as this is security "of" the cloud and, therefore, the responsibility of AWS.

INCORRECT: "Physical network devices including firewalls" arewrong as this is security "of" the cloud and, therefore, the responsibility of AWS.

INCORRECT: "Storage device decommissioning" is incorrect as this is security "of" the cloud and, therefore, the responsibility of AWS.

Question 2Answer: 4

Explanation:

For maximum redundancy and fault tolerance, the application should be deployed in multiple AWS Regions and multiple Availability Zones within each of those regions. This architecture may use Elastic Load

Balancers and Amazon Route 53 records to direct traffic to instances. Alternatively, it could use AWS Global Accelerator.

CORRECT: "Across multiple Availability Zones in two AWS Regions" is the right answer.

INCORRECT: "In a single Availability Zone in one AWS Region" is erroneous as this does not represent the highest redundancy and fault tolerance.

INCORRECT: "In a single Availability Zone in two AWS Regions" is erroneous as this does not represent the highest redundancy and fault tolerance.

INCORRECT: "Across multiple Availability Zones in one AWS Region" is erroneous as this does not represent the highest redundancy and fault tolerance.

Question 3 Answer: 3

Explanation:

Elasticity means that your infrastructure scales based on actual usage. When you have higher demand, you use more infrastructure and pay more, and when you have less request, you need less infrastructure and pay less. The benefits are you don't need to guess about capacity and pay only for what you need.

CORRECT: "Elasticity of the AWS Cloud" is the right answer.

INCORRECT: "Easy global deployments" is erroneous. It is easy to deploy many AWS resources globally. Still, this benefit does not eliminate the need to estimate future usage.

INCORRECT: "Security of the AWS Cloud" is erroneous. The security of the AWS Cloud is essential but does not eliminate the need to estimate future usage.

INCORRECT: "Economies of scale" is erroneous. It means you pay less for some resources because of the benefits of AWS's scale. However, this benefit does not eliminate the need to estimate future usage.

Question 4 Answer: 1, 4

Explanation:

An AWS Managed VPN is a virtual private network connection over the public Internet. It creates an encrypted link between the on-premises network and your AWS VPC.

CORRECT: "AWS Managed VPN" is theright answer.

CORRECT: "AWS Direct Connect" is also theright answer.

Question 5 Answer: 4

Explanation:

You can back up the data on your Amazon EBS volumes to Amazon S3 by taking point-in-time snapshots.

Question 6 Answer: 2

Explanation:

Latency (slow response times) is experienced when resources are far away. Distance is the single most significant factor that causes latency. The easiest option presented to resolve this situation is to place resources closer to where the users are.

CORRECT: "Provision resources in the Asia Pacific (Sydney) Region in Australia" is the right answer.

INCORRECT: "Implement AWS Direct Connect for users in Australia" is erroneous. Direct Connect is a private network connection from your network or data center into a nearby AWS Region. It does not solve the latency issues.

INCORRECT: "Use AWS Transit Gateway to route users from Australia to the application" quickly is wrong. This service is used to connect Amazon Virtual Private Clouds (VPCs) and on-premises networks to a single gateway for connecting multiple VPCs and on-premises systems. It does not solve the latency issues.

INCORRECT: "Launch additional Amazon EC2 instances in Frankfurt to handle the demand" is erroneous. Latency will still be an issue even with more resources in Frankfurt.

Question 7Answer: 4

Explanation:

Only the enterprise plan provides Well-Architected Reviews and Operational Reviews. 24/7 access to Cloud Support Engineers through email, online chat, and the phone is offered on the business and enterprise plans.

CORRECT: "Enterprise" is the right answer.

INCORRECT: "Basic" is erroneous. Basic only includes 24x7 access to customer service, documentation, whitepapers, and support forums.

INCORRECT: "Business" is wrong as it does not provide access to architectural and operational reviews.

INCORRECT: "Developer" is erroneous as you get support from Cloud Support Associates, not Engineers,and also do not get access to architectural and operational reviews.

Question 8 Answer: 2, 4

Explanation:

A couple of the benefits that companies will realize immediately when using the AWS Cloud have increased agility and a change from capital expenditure to variable operational spending.

Agility is enabled through the flexibility of cloud services and the ease with which applications can be deployed, scaled, and managed. When using cloud services, you pay for what you use, and this is a variable, operational expense that can be beneficial to company cashflow.

CORRECT: "Capital expenses are replaced with variable expenses" is theright answer.

CORRECT: "Increased agility" is also theright answer.

INCORRECT: "Variable expenses are replaced with capital expenses" is incorrect. It is the wrong way around; capital expenses are replaced with variable costs.

INCORRECT: "User control of physical infrastructure" is incorrect. It is not true; you do not get control of the physical infrastructure.

Question 9 Answer: 1, 3

Explanation:

Edge Locations are parts of the Amazon CloudFront content delivery network (CDN) that are all around the world and are used to get content closer to end-users for better performance.

AWS Shield, which protects against Distributed Denial of Service (DDoS) attacks, is available globally on Amazon CloudFront Edge Locations.

CORRECT: "Amazon CloudFront" is theright answer.

CORRECT: "AWS Shield" is also theright answer.

INCORRECT: "AWS Direct Connect" is erroneous. AWS Direct Connect is a networking service used for creating a hybrid cloud between on-premises and AWS Cloud using a private network connection

INCORRECT: "Amazon EBS" is erroneous. Amazon EBS is a storage service.

INCORRECT: "AWS Config" is erroneous. AWS Config is used for evaluating the configuration state of AWS resources.

Question 10 Answer: 1

Explanation:

When you deploy an application across multiple Availability Zones, the application can be considered to be highly available. You must also have a way of directing traffic to the application in each AZ, such as an Elastic Load Balancer.

CORRECT: "Being highly available" is the right answer.

INCORRECT: "Having global reach" is incorrect as this refers to deploying applications that can be connected to from around the world and also deploying applications into different regions.

INCORRECT: "Being secure" is incorrect as this is not an example of the implementation of security.

INCORRECT: "Having elasticity" is erroneous. Auto Scaling is an example of elasticity, and it is not mentioned in this question.

Question 11 Answer: 1, 3

Explanation:

AWS Elastic Beanstalk and AWS CloudFormation are both examples of automation. Beanstalk is a platform service that leverages the automation capabilities of CloudFormation to build out application architectures.

CORRECT: "AWS Elastic Beanstalk" is theright answer.

CORRECT: "AWS CloudFormation" is also theright answer.

INCORRECT: "Elastic Load Balancing" is erroneous. Elastic Load Balancing (ELB) is used for distributing incoming connections to Amazon EC2 instances. It is not an example of automation; it is load balancing.

INCORRECT: "Amazon Elastic File System (EFS)" is wrong. Amazon EFS is a file system.

INCORRECT: "AWS Lambda" is erroneous. AWS Lambda is a computing service, not an automation service.

Question 12 Answer: 4

Explanation:

The Business support plan provides a service level agreement (SLA) of < 1 hour for production system down support cases.

CORRECT: "Open a production system down support case" is the right answer.

INCORRECT: "Contact the dedicated Technical Account Manager" is incorrect. The dedicated TAM only comes with the Enterprise support plan.

INCORRECT: "Contact the dedicated AWS Concierge Support team" is incorrect. The concierge support team only comes with the Enterprise support plan.

INCORRECT: "Open a business-critical system down support case" is incorrect. The business-critical system down support only comes with the Enterprise support plan.

Question 13 Answer: 2

Explanation:

Elasticity refers to the automatic scaling of resources based on demand. The benefit is that you provide only the necessary resources at a given time (optimizing cost) and don't have to worry about absorbing spikes in demand.

CORRECT: "By automatically scaling resources based on demand," is the right answer.

INCORRECT: "By reducing interdependencies between application components" is incorrect. Elasticity does not reduce interdependencies between systems – this is known as loose coupling.

INCORRECT: "By selecting the correct storage tier for your workload," is incorrect. Selecting the correct storage tier would be an example of right-sizing, not elasticity.

INCORRECT: "By reserving capacity to reduce cost" is incorrect. Reserving capacity to reduce cost refers to using reservations such as EC2 Reserved Instances.

Question 14 Answer:

Explanation:

Question 15 Answer: 1

Explanation:

An Amazon Virtual Private Cloud (VPC) spans all availability zones within a region.

CORRECT: "Spans all Availability Zones within the region" is the right answer.

Question 16 Answer: 1

Explanation:

AWS Shield Advanced provides enhanced detection and includes a specialized support team for customers on Enterprise or Business support plans. The AWS DDoS Response Team (DRT) is available 24/7 and can be engaged before, during, or after a DDoS attack.

CORRECT: "AWS Shield Advanced" is the right answer.

INCORRECT: "AWS Firewall Manager" is erroneous. This service is used to simplify the management of AWS WAF, AWS Shield Advanced, and Amazon VPC security groups.

INCORRECT: "AWS Web Application Firewall" is incorrect. AWS WAF is used for protecting web applications and APIs against malicious attacks. It is not a DDoS prevention service.

INCORRECT: "Amazon GuardDuty" is incorrect. This service is used for continuously monitoring AWS resources for threats. It is not a DDoS prevention service; it uses machine learning and anomaly detection to identify security vulnerabilities in resources.

Question 17 Answer: 4

Explanation:

A Network ACL is a firewall that is associated with a subnet within your VPC. It is used to filter the network traffic that enters and exits the subnet.

CORRECT: "Network Access Control List" is the right answer.

INCORRECT: "IAM Policy" is incorrect. An IAM policy is used to assign permissions to users and roles.

INCORRECT: "Bucket Policy" is incorrect. A Bucket Policy is used with Amazon S3 buckets to control access.

Question 18 Answer:3, 5

Explanation:

Recovery procedures should always be tested ahead of any outage of a disaster recovery situation.

When designing systems, it is also an excellent practice to implement automatic recovery when possible. It reduces or eliminates the operational burden and potential downtime associated with a failure of a system or application component.

CORRECT: "Testing recovery procedures" is the right answer.

CORRECT: "Automatically recovering from failure" is the right answer.

INCORRECT: "Using monolithic architecture" is incorrect. A monolithic architecture means you have multiple components of an application running on a single system. It results in a more significant issue if that system fails. A distributed architecture is preferred.

INCORRECT: "Measuring overall efficiency" is incorrect. Efficiency has more of a bearing on cost management than reliability.

INCORRECT: "Adopting a consumption model" is wrong. A consumption model has benefits more aligned with cost and agility than reliability.

Question 19 Answer: 1, 5

Explanation:

Subnets and Security groups can be configured from within the VPC console.

CORRECT: "Subnets" is the right answer.

CORRECT: "Security Groups" is the right answer.

Question 20 Answer: 2, 3

Explanation:

IAM groups are used for organizing users and applying policies (permissions) to them. You can add users to multiple groups. Groups cannot be nested, which means you cannot have a group as a member of another group or organize groups in a hierarchy.

CORRECT: "A user can be a member of multiple groups" is theright answer.

CORRECT: "Groups can contain users only and cannot be nested" is also theright answer.

INCORRECT: "Groups can be nested and can contain other groups" is erroneous. You cannot make a group a member of another group or organize them in a hierarchy.

INCORRECT: "A user can only be a member of a single group at one a time" is wrong. It is not true; users can be members of multiple groups.

INCORRECT: "All new users are automatically added to a default group" is erroneous. There is no default group that users are added to when they are created.

Question 21 Answer: 1, 3

Explanation:

You may choose a region to reduce latency, minimize costs, or address regulatory requirements.

Latency is the delay caused mostly by distance. It means you should choose to create your buckets in Regions that are closer (physically) to your users.

Some countries or industries have regulations that mandate data must not leave a jurisdiction or country border. In this case, you simply select an AWS Region accordingly.

Question 22 Answer: 4

Explanation:

Auto Scaling allows the dynamic adjustment of provisioned resources based on demand. For instance, you can use Amazon EC2 Auto Scaling to launch additional EC2 models when CloudWatch metrics report the CPU utilization has reached a certain threshold.

CORRECT: "Auto Scaling" is the right answer.

Question 23 Answer: 3

Explanation:

AWS is responsible for updating Amazon EC2 host firmware. It is considered "security of the cloud." All other tasks are the responsibility of the customer.

CORRECT: "Updating Amazon EC2 host firmware" is the right answer.

INCORRECT: "Granting access to individuals and services" is erroneous. It is something a customer must perform to control access to the resources they use on AWS.

INCORRECT: "Encrypting data in transit" is incorrect. Encryption at rest and in-transit is a customer responsibility.

INCORRECT: "Updating operating systems" is incorrect. Customers are responsible for patching operating systems on Amazon EC2. AWS is only responsible for the host servers.

Question 24 Answer: 3

Explanation:

An Amazon Elastic Block Store (EBS) volume is often described as a "virtual hard disk in the cloud."

CORRECT: "Amazon EBS volume" is the right answer.

INCORRECT: "Amazon EFS Filesystem" is incorrect. An Amazon EFS filesystem is a file-level storage system that is accessed using the NFS protocol. Filesystems are mounted at the file, rather than the block level and are therefore not similar to a virtual hard disk.

INCORRECT: "Amazon S3 Bucket" is incorrect. Amazon S3 is an object-level storage service and is not mounted or attached. You use a REST API over HTTPS to access objects in an object-store.

INCORRECT: "Amazon ENI" is incorrect. An Amazon Elastic Network Interface is a networking construct, not a storage construct.

Question 25 Answer: 3

Explanation:

Amazon EC2 Auto Scaling scales horizontally by adding launching and terminating EC2 instances based on actual demand for your application.

CORRECT: "Horizontal" is the right answer.

INCORRECT: "Vertical" is incorrect as EC2 auto-scaling scales horizontally.

INCORRECT: "Linear" is incorrect as this is not the way Auto Scaling works.

INCORRECT: "Incremental" is incorrect as this is not the way Auto Scaling works.

Billing and Pricing

Question 1 Answer:B

OFFICIAL EXPLANATION:

AWS Secrets Manager is integrated with AWS CloudTrail. This service provides a record of actions taken by a user, role, or an AWS service in Secrets Manager. CloudTrail captures all API calls for Secrets Manager as events, including calls from the Secrets Manager console and code calls to the Secrets Manager APIs.

Question 2 Answer: A, C, D

OFFICIAL EXPLANATION:

The responsibility of AWS includes the following 1) Securing edge locations, 2) Monitoring physical device security, 3) Implementing service organization Control (SOC) standards

Question 3 Answer: A

OFFICIAL EXPLANATION:

The AWS team undertakes the critical measure for providing non-stop monitoring, logging, and auditing of physical access controls.

Question 4 Answer: D

OFFICIAL EXPLANATION:

Through a hybrid cloud, a company can retain control over an internally managed private cloud, while depending on the public cloud, when required. For example, during peak time, you can migrate a few applications to the public cloud.

Question 5 Answer: C

OFFICIAL EXPLANATION:

Provisioned IOPS is used for applications and databases where there is a significant amount of traffic. **Question 6 Answer: C**

OFFICIAL EXPLANATION:

The attributes are also called columns or fields.

Question 7 Answer: D

OFFICIAL EXPLANATION:

AWS Region is another vital feature of the Navigation Bar. If a service supports Regions, the resources in each Region are independent. For example, if you create an Amazon EC2 instance or an Amazon SQS queue in one Region, the model or column is independent of instances or queues in another Region.

Question 8 Answer: C

OFFICIAL EXPLANATION:

Other enterprise applications like databases or ERP systems often require dedicated, low latency storage for each host. This is analogous to direct-attached storage (DAS) or a Storage Area Network (SAN). Block-based cloud storage solutions like Amazon Elastic Block Store (EBS) are provisioned with each virtual server and offer the ultra-low latency required for high-performance workloads.

Question 9 Answer: E

OFFICIAL EXPLANATION:

Screenshot in AWS Doc shows what services the Trusted Advisor Dashboard offers.

Question 10 Answer: B

OFFICIAL EXPLANATION:

The AWS Documentation mentions the following Amazon Simple Notification Service (Amazon SNS) is a web service that enables applications, end-users, and devices to send and receive notifications from the cloud instantly.

Question 11 Answer: D

OFFICIAL EXPLANATION:

Through a hybrid cloud, a company can retain control over an internally managed private cloud, while depending on the public cloud, when required. For example, during peak time, you can migrate a few applications to the public cloud.

Question 12 Answer: C

OFFICIAL EXPLANATION:

Users can access Amazon Web Services through Management Console, Command Line Interface, Command Line Tools, AWS Software Development Kits, and Query APIs.

Question 13 Answer: C

OFFICIAL EXPLANATION:

The C3 instance type offers high-frequency processors for enhanced networking, clustering, and instance storage.

Question 14 Answer: D

OFFICIAL EXPLANATION:

Quickly launch the replacement compute capacity in the cloud for business continuity. After the disaster, restore your data to the data center and terminate the EC2 instances.

Question 15 Answer: C,D

OFFICIAL EXPLANATION:

As per the Shared Responsibility Model, the security for users has to be managed by the AWS Customer.

Question 16 Answer: C

OFFICIAL EXPLANATION:

Since EC2 Instances carry a charge when they are running, you need to factor in the number of servers that need to be migrated to AWS.

Question 17 Answer: A and B

OFFICIAL EXPLANATION:

Full Trusted Advisor Benefits

Business Support and Enterprise Support customers get access to the full set of Trusted Advisor checks and recommendations. It helps optimize your entire AWS infrastructure, increase security and performance, reduce your overall costs, and monitor service limits. Additional benefits include:

Notifications: Stay up-to-date with your AWS resource deployment with weekly updates, plus create alerts and automate actions with Amazon CloudWatch.

Programmatic access: Retrieve and refresh Trusted Advisor results programmatically using AWS Support API.

Question 18 Answer: D

OFFICIAL EXPLANATION:

AWS Lambda service implements the code from Amazon EC2 instances on the virtual servers, in response to a triggered event.

Question 19 Answer: A

OFFICIAL EXPLANATION:

Amazon Route 53, a DNS Web service, is scalable, highly available, and a cost-effective medium to direct the visitors to a website, a virtual server, or a load balancer.

Question 20 Answer: A

OFFICIAL EXPLANATION:

A Load Balancer is responsible for distributing the network traffic across Amazon EC2 instances in different Availability Zones, which enables you to accomplish a higher fault-tolerance level.

Question 21 Answer: D

OFFICIAL EXPLANATION:

AWS Storage Gateway is a scalable and economic amalgamation of your office IT and AWS storage infrastructure.

Question 22 Answer: A

OFFICIAL EXPLANATION:

The disk was the first service offered by Amazon to transfer data using UPS or mail.

Question 23 Answer: B

Question 24 Answer: D

OFFICIAL EXPLANATION:

Designated Technical Account Manager (TAM) to proactively monitor your environment and assist with optimization.

Question 25 Answer: B

OFFICIAL EXPLANATION:

Storing thumbnails & transcoded media is one of the excellent use cases for storing content in AWS RRS, which can be used for later use.

AWS CERTIFIED SOLUTIONS ARCHITECT ASSOCIATE STUDY GUIDE:

THE ULTIMATE CHEAT SHEET PRACTICE EXAM.

QUESTIONS WITH ANSWERS & DETAILED EXPLANATIONS FOR THE LATEST SAA-C01 EXAM

Barry Adams

138

Introduction:

Were you prepared to find out additional? Associate with the AWS engineer network, advance your insight into the web and in-person training, exhibit your ability with confirmations, and investigate reference materials to expand on AWS.

Interface with Engineer Networks

The worldwide AWS environment comprises a scope of AWS fans and backers, who are enthusiastic about helping other people construct.

Client Gatherings

Join an AWS people group close to you to learn, system, and offer distributed computing enthusiasm.

AWS Heroes

Find out about the lively overall network of master clients and influencers.

Virtual People Group

Add your voice to the AWS dialogs occurring in different online networks.

AWS Events

Interface, work together, and gain from specialists on the web and in-person AWS occasions.

Develop Your Range of Abilities

Whether you are only interested in AWS or a prepared star, you have a vast information base.

AWS Online Tech Talks

Stream online introductions and workshops drove by AWS arrangements modelers and specialists.

AWS Partner Network TV

Watch sessions, meetings, demos, and all the more, including AWS and APN Partners.

Get Prepared and Confirmed

Gain from AWS specialists. Advance your aptitudes and information. Manufacture your future in the AWS Cloud.

Computerized and Study Hall Preparing

Learn with free computerized preparing or increase hands-on involvement with a live homeroom.

Accreditation Tests

Acquire qualifications and exhibit your AWS aptitude to bosses and companions.

Investigate Reference Materials

Handy reference materials can help you expand AWS. Before we start, first, let me introduce you to the AWS SAA-C02 exam domain. The examination base on these four domains. Part one is to design Resilient Architectures. Part 2 is to create High-performance Architecture. In domain 3, we will look at how Secure Applications and Architectures can build. Domain 4 is the development of Cost-Optimized Architectures.

Therefore, each of these domains splits into several percentages, i.e., the questions will make up this percentage. For example, Domain one will have 30 percent of the examination. Domain two will cover 28 percent, domain three will have 24 percent, and domain four will have 18 percent of the study. You can see the parts and respective objectives in the following images. It is all about four domains. Let's get started with our prep book.

Domain 1: Design Resilient Architectures 30%

Domain 2: Design High-Performing Architectures 28%

Domain 3: Design Secure Applications and Architectures 24%

Domain 4: Design Cost-Optimized Architectures 18%

TOTAL 100%

Domain 1: Resilient Design Architectures

1.1 Design a multi-tier architecture solution

1.2 Design highly available and fault-tolerant architectures

1.3 Design decoupling mechanisms using AWS services

1.4 Choose appropriate resilient storage

Domain 2: Design High-Performing Architectures

2.1 Identify elastic and scalable compute solutions for a workload

2.2 Select high-performing and scalable storage solutions for a workload

2.3 Select high-performing networking solutions for a workload

2.4 Choose high-performing database solutions for a workload

Domain 3: Design Secure Applications and Architectures

3.1 Design secure access to AWS resources

3.2 Design secure application tiers

3.3 Select appropriate data security options

Domain 4: Design Cost-Optimized Architectures

4.1 Identify cost-effective storage solutions

4.2 Identify cost-effective compute and database services

4.3 Design cost-optimized network architectures

- AWS course and exam resources

- Benefits of becoming on AWS certified solutions architect

Compute

Instance Pricing

Instance, pricing is significant to know when you're looking at cost-optimized compute options in AWS.

On-demand instances: This is good when you have development and test environments and when you want cases for a brief period.

Let's say you have a test environment for a month or a developer environment for say two months; then you should use on-demand

Spot instances: Use this when you have batch processing activities - activities that can survive interruption. We place a high price on the spot instance, and if you lose the bit, you lose the sample. There are other capabilities such as hibernation, but when it comes to the exams, understand that it's only useful when you have batch processing activities to use a spot instance.

Reserved instances: When you know that you need servers 24/7 throughout the year, you can save costs by purchasing reserved capacity.

Dedicated instances: Here, the example runs on hardware that dedicates to a particular customer. It could be a company with multiple AWS accounts, and they have hardware that saves them. If the customer has multiple AWS accounts, then launched across these accounts will share the same hardware.

Dedicated hosts: You have complete control over the physical server. It uses cases where you have a third party application wherein the licensing bases on the number of cores. I have seen applications with a strict policy on licensing that you need to have a physical course as part of the contract; in such a case, you have to use a dedicated host. Or maybe you have a security policy which mandates that you cannot share infrastructure with any other instances; in such a case, you have to use a dedicated host.

Serverless Compute

AWS Lambda

• This is good when you don't want to manage the underlying infrastructure.

• In AWS Lambda, you only get billed for how much of use

• It's effortless to port your existing code and save on the cost by using AWS lambda because you don't need to worry about the costing of your underlying EBS volume or your underlying issue instance.

• Normally, this lambda function is used along with the API gateway; so if you get a question on the combination of services, it's always the API gateway and the AWS lambda.

- You can create APIs in the API gateway service, which can be invoked by customers. Then you can have the APS invoke the lambda functions internally.

Elastic Container Service

It is under operational excellence because we now have microservices, and many organizations are using microservices to design their architecture.

- Elastic container service uses for orchestration of your containers. Instead of installing an orchestration service like Kubernetes on EC2, you can use the elastic container service to manage all the docker containers.

Here you define something known as types; for the kind, you mention the image that needs to pulls down - this could be pulled out from the docker hub or from the elastic container s3, which is available in AWS. It deploys containers on managed instances then you can access all of this via service.

It is all done automatically for you in the elastic container service, as it's a fully managed service. It also has auto-scaling capabilities. If you want orchestration to be handled entirely for you with auto-scaling capabilities, you have to use the Elastic Container Service.

REVIEW QUESTIONS

Question 1:

When the object uploads to the Amazon S3 bucket, you want to run some code. How do I do this?

1. Create an event notification on the S3 bucket that triggered the Lambda function

2. Configure Lambda to poll the S3 bucket for changes and run a role when it finds new objects

3. Create an event notification on the S3 bucket to notify Amazon SNS to trigger the Lambda function

Question 2:

Which type of Amazon storage service uses a standards-based REST web interface to manage objects?

1. Amazon Elastic File System (EFS)

2. Amazon Elastic Block Store (EBS)

3. Amazon Simple Storage Service (S3)

4. Amazon FSx for Windows File Server

Question 3:

Which EC2 pricing model would you use for a short-term requirement that needs to complete over a weekend?

1. Reserved Instance

2. Spot Instance

3. Dedicated Instance

4. On-Demand Instance

Question 4:

How do you create a hierarchy that mimics the file system in Amazon S3?

1. Create buckets within other buckets

2. Use folders in your buckets

3. Upload objects within other objects

4. Use lifecycle rules to tier your data

Question 5:

A new application requires a database that can write to DB instances in multiple availability zones with reading after write consistency. Which solution meets these requirements?

1. Amazon Aurora Global Database

2. Amazon Aurora Replicas

3. Amazon Aurora Cross-Region Replicas

4. Amazon Aurora Multi-Master

Question 6:

A customer needs a schema-less database that can seamlessly scale. Which AWS database service would you recommend?

1. Amazon DynamoDB

2. Amazon ElastiCache

3. Amazon RDS

4. Amazon Aurora

Question 7:

Which DynamoDB feature integrates with AWS Lambda to automatically execute functions in response to table updates?

1. DynamoDB Global Tables

2. DynamoDB Auto Scaling

3. DynamoDB Streams

4. DynamoDB DAX

Question 8:

Which of the following is a fair use case for Amazon RedShift?

1. Schema-less transactional database

2. Relational data warehouse

3. Relational transactional database

4. Analytics using the Hadoop framework

Question 9:

Which Amazon ElastiCache engine provides data persistence?

1. Redis

2. Memcached

Question 10:

At what level do you attach the Internet gateway?

1. Public Subnet

2. Private Subnet

3. Availability Zone

4. VPC

Question 11:

What is the scope of the virtual private cloud (VPC)?

1. Global

2. Regional

3. Availability Zone

Question 12:

The architect needs to point the domain name dctlabs.com to the DNS name of Elastic Load Balancer. Which record type should use?

1. MX record

2. A record

3. CNAME record

4. Alias record

Question 13:

Which of the following listener/protocol combination is incorrect?

1. Application Load Balancer TCP and HTTP/HTTPS

2. Classic Load Balancer TCP and HTTP/HTTPS

3. Network Load Balancer TCP

Question 14:

What type of scaling does Amazon EC2 Auto Scaling provide?

1. Vertical

2.Horizontal

Question 15:

An organization needs a private, high-bandwidth, low-latency connection to the AWS Cloud to establish a hybrid cloud configuration with its on-premises cloud. What type of relationship should they use?

1.   AWS Managed VPN

2.   AWS VPN CloudHub

3.   AWS Direct Connect

4.   Transit VPC

Question 16:

An architect is designing a web application that has locations in multiple regions around the world. The architect wants to provide automatic routing to the nearest area and can failover to other areas. The customer should obtain 2 IP addresses for the whitelist. How do I do this?

1.   Use Route 53 latency-based routing

2.   Use Amazon CloudFront

3.   Use AWS Global Accelerator

4.   Use Route 53 geolocation routing

Question 17:

What services does Amazon API Gateway use for its public terminals?

1.   AWS Lambda

2.   Amazon CloudFront

3.   Amazon S3

4.   Amazon ECS

Question 18:

A company provides videos for new employees around the world. They need to store the videos in one location and then offer low-latency access for the employees around the world. Which service would be best suited to providing fast access to the content?

1.   Amazon S3

2.   AWS Global Accelerator

3.   Amazon CloudFront

4.   AWS Lambda

Storage

Amazon S3 (Simple Storage Service)

These are everything that you will need to manage your data in specific clusters. AWS refers to these clusters of data that you are accessing, caring, and moving as buckets. You will effectively designate several pieces of information or data as one particular bucket. You can then move that bucket around.

These four storage systems are Amazon Standard Storage, Amazon Infrequent Access Storage, Amazon Glacier, and Amazon Reduced Redundancy Storage.

Amazon Standard Storage

It is perfect for data that you need quick access to and is readily available. For example, you may want specific media files used regularly to stores within Amazon Standard Storage, thanks to how readily available and cheap storage is. This data can manage within Amazon Standard Storage. It means that your bill will be based entirely on how much information you use rather than having to buy a specific amount and worrying about data caps.

Amazon Infrequent Access Storage

Resources that you still require for functioning that are less frequently accessed can stores in Amazon Infrequent Access Storage. Data stored here is always readily available but is stored far cheaper. Unlike Amazon Standard Storage, which has an availability of 99.99% of the time (which calculates to less than an hour of downtime within a year), Amazon Infrequent Access Storage is readily available 99.9% of the time, making it down for less than 9 hours a year. If those extra 8 hours of downtime a year are not a concern for you, using Amazon Infrequent Access Storage instead can be a way to save some money.

Amazon Glacier

This third form of data storage allows for the storage of information that is rarely accessed but must be stored. For example, you may use this to keep the work records you rarely need or store backups. It should be information that you will not need instantly. Instead, it should only be for archives of data that you must maintain because it can take significantly longer to retrieve. Think of this data as being stored in a deep freezer— you cannot just instantly thaw it out because you decide you want it right then. Instead, it would help if you waited, and with Amazon Glacier, you sometimes have to wait hours for your archives to thaw out. However, another benefit is that the data stored in Glacier becomes redundant, which means that it is stored in multiple different sites worldwide, allowing you to rest with peace of mind, even in the event of natural disasters or failures in any particular location. You can also use it with confidence.

Amazon Reduced Redundancy Storage

Amazon Reduced Redundancy Storage is meant to store easily reproducible data and is not considered essential to functioning. It is data that is readily available without any real redundancy. It means that it is more vulnerable to loss than the other forms, but it also allows for cheaper storage.

Elastic Block Store

AWS Elastic Block Store (EBS) allows for the storage volumes to provide low latency. The range of workloads provides for several different processes to be included and possible with EBS, such as:

• Relational and non-relational databases

• Containerized applications

• File systems

• Enterprise applications

• Data analytics engines

When utilizing EBS, you give the option between four different types that will allow you to choose an option that balances your price range with the performance you wish to achieve. You will see functions and systems that can process data nearly instantly with single digit-millisecond latency. EBS can find in four forms: General Purpose SSD, Provisioned IOPS SSD, Throughput Optimized HDD, and Cold HDD.

Snowball

The recommended solution for moving the most amounts of on-premises data to the AWS cloud as fast as possible is AWS Snowball. It is an appliance-based storage device shipped to the tenant where up to 50 TB data can be loaded. The appliance sends back to the tenant where

AWS receives it and copies data over AWS S3 storage. There is support for multiple devices with concurrent data transfers and 256-bit encryption of data at rest. Snowball recommendsreplacing AWS Import/Export, particularly with data transfers larger than 10 TB to S3 buckets. Snowball jobs create from the AWS management console, and a Snowball appliance is automatically shipped on-premises.

Elastic File System (EFS)

Elastic File System enables what is essentially a file server in the Cloud. The EFS is associated with a single VPC where users with security permissions can access and share files. The Elastic File System is a managed service created and mounted on single or multiple Linux-based EC2 instances to enable data file storage and sharing. EFS provides file locking and strong consistency that is characteristic of a file system. There is also support for mounting EFS file systems within your VPC to any on-premises servers for migrating, backup, or workload purposes. It allows thousands of EC2 instances to upload, access, delete, and share files simultaneously.

AWS Storage Gateway

Amazon AWS Storage Gateway is a hybrid solution that supports storing some or all of the data locally to improve performance. AWS Storage Gateway is a software (virtual) device deployed locally that provides native encryption of tenant data.The following is a list of AWS storage gateway options that store some or all cloud data.

• Stored Volume Gateway

- Cached Volume Gateway

- Tape Gateway (VTL)

REVIEW QUESTIONS

Question 1

For non-relational databases,which is the best AWS Service?

Choose one out of four.

A.   Amazon Glacier

B.   Amazon DynamoDB

C.   Amazon Redshift

D.   Amazon RDS

Question 2

Amazon ElastiCache supports which of the following cache engines?

Choose two out of four.

A.   Memcached

B.   Couchbase

C.   MySQL

D.   Redis

Question 3

From the actions below, which IAM policies can control ones?

Choose three out of five.

A.   Creating an Amazon S3 bucket

B.   Logging into .NET applications

C.   Creating tables in a MySQL RDS database

D.   Configuring a VPC security group

E.   Creating an Oracle RDS database

Question 4

A t2.medium EC2 instance type launches with what kind of Amazon Machine Image (AMI)?

A. An Instance store Hardware Virtual Machine AMI

B. An Instance store Paravirtual AMI

C. An Amazon EBS-backed Hardware Virtual Machine AMI

D. An Amazon EBS-backed Paravirtual AMI

Question 5

To launch a fully configured instantly, what is the template that Auto Scaling would use?

Choose one out of four.

A.   User data

B.   Launch configuration

C.   Keypair

D.   Instance type

Question 6

Of the options below, which are characteristics of the AWS Auto Scaling Service?

Choose two out of six.

A.   Collects and tracks metrics and sets alarms

B.   Delivers push notifications

C.   Sends traffic to healthy instances

D.   Enforces a minimum number of running Amazon EC2 instances

E.   Responds to changing conditions by adding or terminating Amazon EC2 instances.

F.   Launches instances from a specified Amazon Machine Image (AMI).

Question 7

A customer needs a file, such as a PDF file made available to be publicly downloadable. The PDF file is going to be downloaded by customers using their browsers. The PDF file will be downloaded in this manner millions of times. From the options below, which will be the most cost-effective for the customer?

Choose one out of four.

A.   Store the file in Glacier

B.   Store the file in EFS

C.   Store the file in S3 Standard

D.   Store the file in S3 Standard-IA

Question 8

A mobile phone application runs statistical articles from individual files in an Amazon S3 bucket. There are articles older than 40 days that no more extended needs for the application and items over 30 days old that are hardly ever read. These articles are no longer required to be visible through the mobile application. Still, the archive for historical data purposes.

From the list below, select the cost-effective solution that best meets these requirements.

Choose one out of four.

A.   For files older than 30 days, create lifecycle rules to move these files to Amazon S3 Standard Infrequent Access and use Amazon Glacier to move files older than 40 days.

B.   For files more aged than 30 days, create a Lambda function to force them to Amazon Glacier and move files older than 40 days to Amazon EBS.

C.   Create a Lambda function that moves files to Amazon EBS that are older than 30 days and transfer files to Amazon Glacier older than 40 days.

D.   For files more aged than 30 days, create lifecycle rules to move these files to Amazon Glacier and use Amazon S3 Standard Infrequent Access to move files older than 40 days to.

Question 9

A Solutions Architect is designing a log-processing solution that requires storage that supports up to 500 MB/s throughput. An Amazon EC2 instance sequentially accesses the data.

Which Amazon storage type satisfies these requirements?

Choose one out of four.

A.   EBS Cold HDD (sc1)

B.   EBS Provisioned IOPS SSD (io1)

C.   EBS General Purpose SSD (gp2)

D.   EBS Throughput Optimized HDD (st1)

Networking

VPC sizing and structure

VPC consideration

• How big should the VPC be. It will limit usage.

• Are there networks that cannot use?

• Pay attention to the ranges used by other VPCs or used in different cloud environments.

• Try to predict future uses.

• VPC structure with levels and zones of resilience (availability)

• VPC min/28 network (16 IP)

• VPC max /16 (65456 IP)

How to size VPC

A subnet is in an availability zone. Try to divide each subnet into levels (application, web, database, reservation). Since each region has at least three AZs, it is good to separate the network into four different AZs. It allows at least one subnet in each AZ and one reservation. Taking a /16 subnet and dividing it into 16 shapes will make each one a /20.

VPC subnets

AZ Strong VPC subnet.

• If the Available zone fails, the subnet and services also fail.

- High availability requires multiple components in different AZs.

- One subnet can only have 1 AZ.

- 1 AZ can have zero or more subnets.

- CIDR IPv4 is a subset of the VID CIDR block.

- Impossible to overlap with other subnets in that VPC

- Optionally, the IPv6 CIDR block can assign to the subnet.

- (256/64 subnets can adapt to /56 VPC)

- Subnets can interact with other subnets in the VPC by default.

VPC Routing and Internet Gateway

VPC Router is a high availability device available in every VPC that moves traffic from one place to another. The router has a network interface on each subnet of the VPC. Route traffic between subnets. Routing tables define what the VPC router will do with the traffic when the data leaves that subnet. A VPC creates a primary route table. If a custom route table is not associated with a subnet, it uses the main route table of the VPC.

NAT - Network Address Translation Gateway

Set of diverse processes that can address IP packets by alternating their source or destination addresses. It allows many IPv4 lessons to use a public IP for outgoing access to the Internet. Incoming connections don't work. Outgoing links can get a returned response.

- It must be run from a public subnet to allow the public IP address.

o Internet Gateway subnets configure to assign available IPv4 addresses and default routes for those subnets that point to IGW.

• Use elastic IP (public static IPv4)

o Do not change

o Assigned to your account

• Resilient service AZ, but HA in that AZ.

o If that Available zon=e fails, there is no recovery.

REVIEW QUESTIONS

Question 1:

On Friday morning, your marketing manager calls an urgent meeting to celebrate that they have secured a deal to run a coordinated national promotion on TV, radio, and social media over the next ten days. They anticipate a 500x increase in site visits and trial registrations. After the meeting, you throw some ideas around with your team about ensuring that your current one server web site will survive. Which of these best embodies the AWS design strategy for this situation? [Select 2]

A) Work with your web design team to create web pages with embedded java scripts to emulate your five most popular information web pages and sign up web pages.

B) Upgrade your existing server from a 1xlarge to a 32xlarge for the duration of the campaign.

C) Create a stand by sign up a server to use if the primary fails due to load.

D) Create a duplicate sign up page that stores registration details in DynamoDB for asynchronous processing using SQS & Lambda.

E) Work with your web design team to create web pages in PHP to run on a 32xlarge EC2 instance to emulate your five most popular information web pages and sign up web pages.

F) Recreate your five most popular new customer web pages and sign up web pages on LightSail and take advantage of AWS auto-scaling to pick up the load.

Question 2:

A software development company has recently invested 20 million dollars in building their artificial intelligence APIs and AI-powered chatbots. You are hired as a Solutions Architect to build a low-cost prototype on their AWS cloud infrastructure. Which of the following AWS service combinations will provide user authentication, scalable object storage, and allow you to run code without having to host it in an EC2 instance?

A) Cognito, Lambda, S3

B) AWS IoT, Cognito, S3

C) IAM, Lambda, EBS Volumes

D) IAM, Cognito, EBS Volumes

Question 3:

When using EC2 instances with Dedicated Hosting, which of the following modes are you able to transition between by stopping the model and starting it again?

A) Dedicated & Default

B) Non-Dedicated & Dedicated

C) Host & Default

D) Dedicated & Host

Question 4:

Which of the following are valid Route 53 routing policies? [Select 3]

A) Latency

B) Multitarget answer

C) Simple

D) Weighted

E) Complex

F) Shortest First

Question 5:

You have an EC2 instance that is transferring data from S3 in the same region. The project sponsor is worried about the cost of the infrastructure. What can you do to convince him that you have a cost-effective solution?

A) You are going to be hosting only four instances, so you are minimizing cost.

B) There is no cost for transferring data from EC2 to S3 if they are in the same region.

C) AWS provides a discount if you transfer data from EC2 to S3 if they are in the same region.

D) Both EC2 and S3 are in the same availability zone so that you can save via consolidated billing.

Question 6:

What are the data formats used to create CloudFormation templates? [Select 2]

A) XML

B) YAML

C) CSV

D) JSON

Question 7:

A company has a solution hosted in AWS. This solution consists of a set of EC2 instances. They have been recently getting attacks as their IT security departments identified that attacks are from a group of IP addresses. Which of the following methods can be adopted to help in this situation?

A) Place the EC2 instances into private subnets and set up a NAT gateway so employees can access them.

B) Remove the IGW from the VPC so that no outside traffic can reach the EC2 instances.

C) Lockdown of NACL for the set to IP address.

D) Place the EC2 instances into private subnets and set up a bastion host so employees can access them.

Question 8:

Which of the following Amazon S3 Storage Classes offer 99.999999999% (11 x 9s) durability?

A) Standards are not frequently accessed, and an area is not frequently accessed, reducing redundant storage

B) Standard, Standard-Infrequent Access, One Zone-Infrequent Access

C) Reduced Redundancy Storage, Standard, One Zone-Infrequent Access

D) Standard, Glacier, Reduced Redundancy Storage

Question 9:

You work for a genomics company developing a cure for motor neuron disease by using advanced gene therapies. As a part of their research, they take massive data sets (usually in the terabytes) and analyze these data sets using Elastic Map Reduce. To keep costs low, they run the analysis for only a few hours in the early hours of the morning, using spot instances for the task nodes. The core nodes are on-demand instances.

Lately, however, the EMR jobs have been failing. It is due to spot instances unexpectedly terminate. Which of the following remedies would keep costs manageable and mitigate the issues caused by terminated spot instances? [Select 2]

A) Change the core nodes to spot cases and lower the spot price.

B) Increase the bid price for the core nodes.

C) Change the task nodes to on-demand instances.

D) Increase the bid price for the task nodes to have a more significant threshold before the task nodes terminate.

Question 10:

Amazon Web Services offers four different levels of support. Which of the following are reasonable support levels? [Select 3]

A) Business

B) Enterprise

C) Developer

D) Corporate

E) Free Tier

Question 11:

Which of the following AWS services encrypts data at rest by default? (Choose 2)

A) AWS Storage Gateway

B) Amazon RDS

C) Amazon DynamoDB

D) Amazon Glacier

Question 12:

You work for a large software company in Seattle.

They configured a production environment on AWS on a custom VPC. VPC includes public subnets and private subnets.

The company tests its applications on custom EC2 instances in a private subnet.

There are approximately 500 instances, and they communicate to the outside world via a proxy server. At 3am every night, the EC2 instances pull-down OS updates, usually 150MB or so. They then apply these updates and reboot: if the software has not downloaded within half an hour, the update will attempt to download the following day.

Which of the following answers might explain this failure? [Select 2]

A) Your proxy server is blacklisting the address from which the updates download, resulting in failed downloads.

B) The proxy server is located in a private subnet and uses a NAT instance to connect to the Internet.However, this instance is too small to handle the required network traffic. You should re-provision the NAT solution so that it's able to handle the throughput.

C) The proxy server has only one elastic IP address added to it. To increase network throughput, you should add additional elastic IP addresses.

D) The proxy server has an inadequately sized EBS volume attached to it. The network buffer stores on the EBS volume, and it is running out of disk space when trying to ease the 500 simultaneous connections. You should provision an EBS volume with provisioned IOPS.

E) The proxy server is on an inadequately sized EC2 instance.

It does not have sufficient network throughput to handle all updates simultaneously. You should increase the instance size or type of the EC2 model for the proxy server.

Question 13:

Which of the following AWS services allow native encryption of data while at rest? [Select 3]

A) ElastiCache for Memcached

B) Elastic Block Store (EBS)

C) S3

D) Elastic File System (EFS)

Question 14:

You are consulting with a mid-sized company with a predominantly Mac & Linux desktop environment. In passing, they comment that they have over 30TB of unstructured Word and spreadsheet documents, of which

85% of these documents don't get accessed again after about 35 days. They wish they could find a quick and easy solution to have tiered storage to store these documents more cost-effectively without impacting staff access. What options can you offer them? [Select 2]

A) Migrate documents to File Gateway presented as iSCSI and made use of life-cycle using Infrequent Access storage.

B) Migrate the document store to S3 storage and make use of life-cycle using Infrequent Access storage.

C) Migrate documents to EFS storage and make use of life-cycle using Infrequent Access storage.

D) Migrate documents to File Gateway presented as NFS and made use of life-cycle using Infrequent Access storage.

Question 15:

A single m4. Medium NAT instance inside a VPC supports a company of 100 people. This NAT instance allows individual EC2 models in private subnets to communicate out to the internet without being directly accessible via the internet. As the company has grown over the past year, they have discovered that the additional traffic passing through the NAT instance is causing severe performance degradation. What might you do to solve this problem?

A) Instead of using a NAT, use Direct Connect to route all traffic through your VPC and back out to the Internet.

B) Attach an additional IGW to your VPC.

C) Increase the class size of the NAT instance from an m4.medium to an m4.xLarge.

D) Use an Elastic Load Balancer and forward traffic out through this ELB. The ELB will automatically scale on-demand as traffic increases.

Content delivery

Amazon Route 53

Amazon Route 53 is the built-in AWS DNS service. It is responsible for the time and price-efficient routing of DNS (domain name system). The internet can convert the URL into a web browser into an IP address associated with that URL. Effectively, this is the program that will allow for access to the webpages.

Route 53 design work in tandem with other AWS infrastructure—in particular, it is efficient when utilized with;

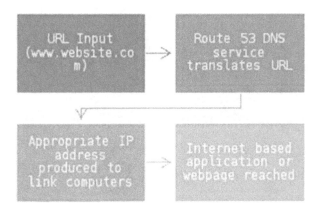

Amazon EC2 instances

- ELB load balancers

- Amazon S3 buckets

- Outside infrastructure

Thanks to its flexibility, you can use Route 53 to make sure that traffic makes it to the proper endpoint, as well as to monitor whether requests redirect appropriately, arriving at their endpoint without issue. There are several other functions to keep track of and manage traffic on your domain, such as:

• Latency based routing: Route 53 balances out the traffic load so that latency does not overwhelm one or two endpoints.

• GeoDNS: You can route customers to specific domains based on the customer's location based on the location services within the device used.

• Geoproximity: Users will be routed based on the physical distance between the user and the resources, causing users to access the closest data center.

• Weighted round-robin: You will be able to specify specific weights or traffic loads that can be handled by each server, route more traffic that can operate without overwhelming servers that not be able to withstand the same traffic.

The above information is stored in the program Amazon Route 53 Traffic Flow, which allows you to perform all monitoring in one place. It can also be used in conjunction with DNS failover to achieve a low-latency and fault-tolerant architecture to keep servers and domains running.As one last point, Amazon Route 53 also provides for domain name registration. You can directly purchase your domain names through AWS, and Route 53 will take care of configuring the DNS settings for you.

CloudFront

Amazon CloudFront allows the delivery of content globally. It utilizes the massive global infrastructure that Amazon has built up to provide high speed and low cost. It will enable the content to keep closer to the user than ever, allowing for a better experience using the products, thanks to receiving content quicker than ever. Virtually, its design to be low-latency with a high transfer rate while also being incredibly developer-friendly. It is built into AWS and works smoothly and effectively with all other AWS products and services. Even better, if you are already using AWS origins for the data, such as having it processed from Amazon S3, EC2, or ELB, you will not have to pay for the transfer of data from those services CloudFront instance you are using.

This service comes with several key benefits that make it fantastic to utilize your AWS services:

• Global without sacrificing speed: It utilizes global distribution on a massive scale, with 200 points of presence while relying on Amazon's network for wide availability for the users of your programs or websites.

• Secure: Despite several security concerns, CloudFront is mostly secure, with both in-network protection and protection on the application level. It includes Amazon Shield Standard with the program itself and configurable settings, such as AWS Certificate Manager and custom SSL certificates, without spending extra.

• Customizable: It is mainly programmable and customizable to fit what your application requires. Your code can be spread across several

176

AWS locations worldwide to increase response times and integrate it with several other tools.

•   Already integrated within AWS: Thanks to being a part of the AWS arsenal, it connects with other AWS services. Your CloudFront operations can be accessed in the same console as your other AWS services, making it a popular choice.

CloudWatch

The last of the AWS Essential services is CloudWatch. It is effectively your monitoring hub. When you use CloudWatch, you can monitor the AWS applications that you are utilizing. It allows you to see statistics and usage in near-real-time for your essential services, such as:

•   Amazon Elastic Compute Cloud instances

•   Amazon Elastic Block Store volumes

•   Amazon Relational Database Service

•   Elastic Load Balancers

It works because it can collect data, monitor your applications and infrastructure, act accordingly, and analyze your AWS infrastructure, services, and applications.

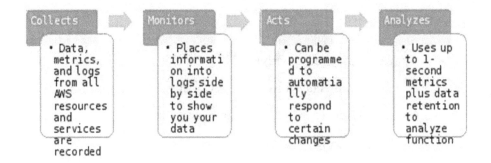

Collects	Monitors	Acts	Analyzes
• Data, metrics, and logs from all AWS resources and services are recorded	• Places informati on into logs side by side to show you your data	• Can be programme d to automatia lly respond to certain changes	• Uses up to 1-second metrics plus data retention to analyze function

Thanks to the fact that it automatically integrates with AWS, you are set up to use it quickly and simply, allowing you to read statistics and metrics on latency, the current usage of CPU, request counts, and more. You will be able to track the health of your application, the number of resources used, any issues that may arise, and any restrictions encountered.

Because you have all of this information readily available, you can solve any IT issues that come up with ease.

CloudWatch is mainly integrated into EC2, providing two different levels of monitoring based on what works best for you. These are:

• Basic Monitoring: No added fees—this also includes seven metrics of your choice that runs every 5 minutes, and three status-check metrics run every 1 minute.

• Detailed Monitoring: Has added fees—this allows you to make sure that all metrics increase to occurring in 1-minute intervals.

Beyond just that, CloudWatch monitors the following:

178

- Latency within EBS

- Storage space and freeable memory metrics within the RDS database

- Messages sent and received within SQS queues

- The number of delivered messages through SNS topics

CloudWatch can also be customized to provide the client with a graph of data within AWS services—both real-time and data logged over the last two weeks. It is also possible to create alarms and notifications whenever any metrics are outside of specified ranges and when resources did not utilize to their potential. It can even involve customizing some specific responses to certain parameters that can automatize.

REVIEW QUESTIONS

Question 1

Which of the following options enables users to access private files in S3 in a secure manner? (Choose three)

a)   CloudFront-origin access identity

b)   CloudFront-signed URLs

c)   Public S3 buckets

d)   CloudFront-signed cookies

Question 2

Which is not part of a Cloud Adoption Framework component?

a)   Creation of a strong business case for cloud adoption

b)   Incentive and career management aligned with evolving roles

c)   Identity and access management modes change

d)   Align KPIs with newly-enabled business capabilities

e)   Reinvent business processes to take advantage of new capabilities

Question 3

AWS CloudFront Distribution types are _____. (Select two)

a)   Horizontal

b)   Web

c)   RTMP

d)   All of the above

Question 4

To restrict any user belonging to a specific country from accessing the content, which features of AWS CloudFront use?

a)   CNAME

b)   Geo-restriction

c)   Zone apex

d)   Invalidation

Question 5

AWS CloudFront can work with the non-origin server as well. True or false?

a)   True

b)   False

Question 6

Which features of AWS CloudFront can you use to remove malicious or harmful objects before its expiration time from all edge locations?

a)   CNAME

b)   Zone Apex

c)   Invalidation

d)   Geo-restriction

Question 7

In AWS CloudFront, you can use SSL via a default URL or a custom URL. For a custom URL, you can use two types of configuration. Name them by selecting any two from the following options.

a)   Dedicated IP Custom SSL

b)   SNI Custom SSL

c)   Custom SSL using Cloudflare

d)   Custom SSL with Azure

Question 8

What are the HTTP methods that donot cache in CloudFront Edge Location?

a)   PUT, POST, PATCH, and DELETE

b)   PUT, POST, PATCH, and GET

c)   PUT, GET, OPTION, and DELETE

d)   HEAD, POST, PATCH, and GET

Question 9

Amazon Route 53 does not perform _____.

a)   Health checks

b)   Domain registration

c)   Load balancing

d)   DNS services

Question 10

What is the use of the Subnet Associations tab in a VPC route table?

Databases

The database instance includes all compute and storage attributes assigned to a database/s. It defines all components and settings of a full-fledged database environment.

Amazon AWS tenants often have multiple database instances for high availability and failover purposes assigned to a private subnet. The tenant must give a security group to a database instance. Also, the DNS hostname and DNS resolution attribute configured to resolve DNS requests.

Amazon RDS

Managed Services

It designs to provide database ready services to tenants with minimal setup. The tenant is responsible for any application-level configuration, security groups, and IAM policies. VPC security groups enable EC2 instances and RDS instances to share the same security group within a VPC. The purpose is to control access to database instances and EC2 instances inside a VPC. EC2 security groups, by contrast, control access to an EC2 model only.

Amazon installs instances, allocates capacity, and performs backups, failovers, and data replication. The tenant cannot use the SSH root directory to access the database instance.

183

Each database instance can contain tables created by multiple users. Amazon RDS uses Elastic Block Storage (EBS) volumes for database and logs storage.

The allocated storage can increase with various striped EBS volumes.

Read Replica

RDS enables horizontal scaling with reading replicas that allow you to scale out as database workloads increase elastically. Multiple read requests route (split) among readingimages to improve throughput and lower latency for average and peak traffic events. Adding read replicas to an RDS managed database would increase database capacity through the number of transactions per second. The effect of horizontal scaling is to distribute packets across multiple database instances. Read replicas are read-only copies that synchronize with a source (master) database instance.

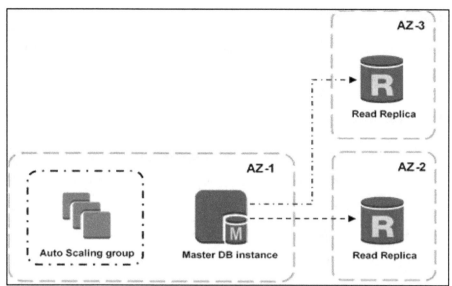

The source database is encrypted at rest and in transit for reading replications to slave databases within the Cloud. Any read replication requires selecting a target region and encryption key for the target region. You can use your passport or default key generated by KVM in the target region.

The source database sends only read-only replica updates after the initial synchronization to the slave database/s has occurred. There is currently support for up to five in-region and cross-region replicas supported per API call. Also, Amazon permits a maximum of 40 RDS database instances.

Amazon Redshift

RedShift is well suited for warehousing and analyzing Petabyte amounts of data to run SQL analytical tools. RedShift aims to provide a data warehouse solution where tenants can run sophisticated SQL queries and Business Intelligence reporting tools in real-time or offline. RedShift analyses behaviors, patterns, and trends for gaming, stocks, logs, twitter, sensor data, and clickstreams.

Amazon Aurora

Amazon Aurora is a cost-effective open-source relational database that is fully managed by RDS. It is an enhancement to MySQL and PostgreSQL compatible RDS. It is five times faster than a standard MySQL database, has shorter recovery times, and has minimal replication latency. It provides security, fault tolerance, and durability of commercial databases at 10%.Amazon DynamoDB

Standard Features

DynamoDB is a NoSQL managed database service deployed for applications that require fast concurrent read/write lookups for smaller records with low latency (msec). Also, DynamoDB is well suited to store and retrieval of frequently accessed records. It supports multiple store models, such as documents and key-value. There is virtually unlimited scalability that adds automatically based on throughput and storage requirements.

Capacity Management

DynamoDB supports a feature called Auto Scaling that allows tenants to configure a range of capacity units with a maximum value. That enables capacity units to be increased temporarily during periods of peak traffic and prevent throttling.

DynamoDB publishes capacity metrics to CloudWatch, and any exceeded event triggers a CloudWatch alarm and SNS notification. The notice then invokes the Auto Scaling feature within DynamoDB to increase or decrease capacity units.

Amazon ElastiCache

Data Store Caching

Amazon ElastiCache is a fast in-memory caching service. It allows tenants to store frequently accessed data from multiple data stores. This strategy can reduce the processing burden to optimize data access time. The result is lower latency and response time, which speeds up queries. There is less durability, however, when compared with native database access. Amazon AWS supports the popular Memcached and Redis caching engines. It is a managed service that offloads the deployment, maintenance, and administration of caching software from tenants to the Cloud.

REVIEW QUESTIONS

Question 1:

Your new educational app for high-school students uses Amazon Cognito to handle user authentication and authorization. Now, you are thinking of adding another method of authentication and just a username and password to make the app more secure. What solution will you implement to add the extra layer of security?

(A) Add Social sign-in with Facebook, Google

(B) Add multi-factor authentication (MFA) with a Cognito user pool

(C) Add sign-in with SAML identity providers

187

(D) Integrate IAM with the user pool in Cognito.

Question 2:

You have hosted your new application in an Auto Scaling group of EC2 instances. Now you need to implement an SSL solution for your system to improve its security. The certificate obtains from a third-party issuer. Where can you 161

import the SSL/TLS certificate to enhance the security of your application?

(A) Amazon CloudFront

(B) AWS CloudHSM

(C) AWS Security Hub

(D) AWS Certificate Manager

Question 3:

Which of the following VPC features copies the network traffic from an elastic network interface of an Amazon EC2 instance and send the traffic to monitoring appliances?

(A) Flow logs

(B) Traffic mirroring

(C) Network access control lists (ACLs) (D) Security groups

Question 4:

Which of the following caching engines support on Amazon Elasticache? (Choose two answers)

A.   CouchBase

B.   Varnish

C.   Xcache

D.   Memcached

E.   Redis

Question 5:

Which of the following ACL rules allows inbound 38?

HTTP traffic from any IPv4 address.

(A) Rule: 100, Type: HTTP, Protocol: TCP, Port range: 80, Source: 0.0.0.0/0, Allow/Deny: ALLOW

(B) Rule: 100, Type: HTTP, Protocol: TCP, Port range: 443, Source: 0.0.0.0/0, Allow/Deny: ALLOW

(C) Rule: 100, Type: HTTP, Protocol: TCP, Port range: 53, Source: 0.0.0.0/0, Allow/Deny: ALLOW

(D) Rule: 100, Type: HTTP, Protocol: TCP, Port range: 22, Source: 0.0.0.0/0, Allow/Deny: ALLOW

Question 6:

ABC Corporation has a successful ERP web application that uses a multi-AZ RDS instance as its database tier. They are working on adding a Business Intelligence (BI) application to their offering to offer advanced reporting and analytic capabilities on their ERP data for their customers. They are worried about the additional workload from the BI application on their database tier. 95% of the BI requests will be 'read' operations on the dataset. Which of the following designs can provide BI applications with access to data without introducing a large amount of work on existing RDS instances? Which method is cost-effective?

A.   Introduce multiple 'read' replicas that replicate and sync with the primary RDS instance. The BI application will send its requests to the 'read' replicas.

B.   Introduce an Elasticache layer to offload requests and cache data from the primary RDS instance. The BI application will send its recommendation to Elasticache.

C.   Introduce an Amazon EMR cluster and copy data to the EMR cluster. The BI application will send its requests to the EMR cluster.

D.   Introduce an Amazon Redshift cluster and copy data from the RDS instance using CodePipeline or DMS to keep data in sync. The BI application will send its requests to the Redshift cluster.

Question 7:

Which of the following can serve as an origin for HTTP/HTTPS CloudFront distributions? Choose three answers.

A.   Amazon load balancers

B.   Amazon S3 bucket

C.   An on-premises web server

D.   Adobe media server on EC2 instance

E.   Wowza streaming server on EC2 instance

F.   Elasticache instance

Question 8:

You are developing an application that uses Python Lambda functions. You need to store some sensitive data such as credentials for accessing the database. How will you keep this data securely and adjust your function's behavior without updating code?

(A) Use AWS Lambda environment variables (B) Use AWS Identity and Access Management (C) Use AWS CloudTrail

(D) Use AWS CodeDeploy

Question 9:

You are working for a content management company as an AWS Architect. The company needs a storage service that provides the scale and performance the content management applications require, such as high throughput and low-latency file operations. Their data needs to be stored redundantly across multiple AZs and allows concurrent connections from numerous EC2 instances hosted on multiple 60AZs. Which of the following AWS storage services is most suitable for the project?

(A) Amazon Elastic Block Store (EBS)

(B) Amazon S3

(C) AWS Storage Gateway

(D) Amazon EFS

Question 10:

You have just created a new **On-Demand EC2 instance located in a subnet with ID subnet-aa181cd0 and IPv4 CIRD 172.31.16.0/20 in AWS, which hosts your WordPress blog site. The security group attached to this EC2 instance has the following inbound rules:**

Inbound rules

Type	Protocol	Port range	Source	Description - opti
HTTP	TCP	80	0.0.0.0/0	examsdigest http
Custom TCP	TCP	20 - 21	0.0.0.0/0	examsdigest ftp co
HTTPS	TCP	443	0.0.0.0/0	examsdigest https

You can establish an FTP connection into the EC2 instance from the internet. However, you are not able to establish an SSH connection from the internet. How to resolve the issue?

(A) In the Security Group, add an Inbound SSH rule

(B) In the Security Group, change FTP's Source IP to 172.31.16.20

(C) In the Security Group, remove the HTTPS rule

(D) In the Security Group, add an Outbound SSH rule

Question 11:

The following AWS Key Management Service practice encrypts plaintext data with a data key. Does it then encrypt the data key under another key?

(A) Key usageKey usage

(B) Envelope encryption

193

(C) Key spec

(D) Cryptographic operations

Question 12:

For storage of complex data types, like strings, which cache engine uses?

a) Redis

b) MySQL

c) No SQL

d) Memcached

Question 13.

Replication and Multi-AZ is one of the best approaches for

_____.

a) Fast recovery

b) Low latency

c) Low availability

d) The increasing effect of loss

Question 14:

When do you need to distribute your data over multiple nodes that the ElastiCache engine used?

a)   Members

b)   Redis

c)   Memcached

Question 15:

Which ElastiCache engine operates for the persistence of crucial stores?

a)   Members

b)   Redis

c)   Memcached

d)   MySQL

Analytics

In addition to all the services and solutions discussed so far, Amazon offers services related to analytics, which help build and manage analytics solutions. Data Lakes, powered by Amazon, ensures the scalability, flexibility, and agility needed to handle more in-depth analytics, which is missing in traditional data warehouses. AWS provides analytics and machine learning services, adhering to governance and security.

AWS offers a set of services to build an analytics solution and data lakes – data movement, data lake, analytics, and machine learning.

Data Movement: Import data from on-premise, real-time

One of the critical services offered by AWS is moving data from on-premise centers to the Cloud. However, there are challenges around the data movement related to bandwidth and transfer speed. Still, AWS ensures easy transfer by providing some of the best options available. There are multiple ways to move data from the local data center to the AWS cloud –

AWS Direct Connect establishes a dedicated network connection between the physical data center and Cloud.

- **AWS Snowball and AWS Snowmobile use when physical entities must use to transfer massive amounts of data (PB to EB).AWS Storage Gateway to store on-premise application data directly on the Cloud.**

Once data is made available for movement, Amazon ensures it can safely store in any required format so that end-users can use it for specific purposes. AWS Glue provides the data that is made searchable and accessible for running queries by storing it in a single catalog.

- **Storage: Amazon provides S3 for object storage – a scalable, securable, and durable option, specially built to store all sorts of data, from any device or application. It can keep any amount of data, without compromising retrieval speed. S3 is also famous for its compliance capabilities and security controls.**

- **Data Catalog: Amazon provides AWS Glue service to make data discoverable and searchable in the data lake. This managed service can extract, transform, and load data for analysis purposes. Data catalog created for data assets makes the data searchable and queryable.**

- **Data Archive and Backup: Amazon Glacier is the service offered by Amazon for data archival and backup. It is a secure and low-cost storage option that can use as a long-term backup and archive. It can access data in a few minutes and designto meetthe compliance capabilities and security requirements.**

Analytics and Data Warehousing

AWS provides the most effective and low-cost analytics service to analyze data stored in data lakes. These services design for various analytics purposes, such as big data processing, interactive analysis, real-time analytics, visualizations,etc.

- **Big Data Processing:** Amazon brings to its users Amazon EMR that helps in big data processing with the help of frameworks such as Hadoop. It is a managed service capable of processing vast data in a practical, quick, and cost-effective manner.

- **Interactive analysis:** Amazon Athena is another analytics service that analyzes the data stored in S3 and Glacier by running standard SQL queries. Since it is serverless, there is no infrastructure required to manage or set up this service.

- **Real-time analytics:** Amazon Kinesis is the service offered by Amazon for real-time analysis. It accesses, processes, and analyzes streaming data, such as application log data, IoT data, etc., efficiently and in real-time. Therefore, the need to wait until the information is collected eliminates.

- **Visualizations and dashboards:** Amazon provides QuickSight for dashboards and visualizations. It is a cloud-based analytics service that helps to build great visualizations and dashboards that can use from any device or application.

- **Data Warehousing: Amazon Redshift is the data warehousing service provided by Amazon to its users. It can run complex queries to analyze petabytes of data. This service includes Redshift Spectrum that runs complex queries to analyze exabytes of data stored in S3.**

We read about data lakes, but do we know how lakes form?

AWS Lake Formation is an Amazon service that helps in setting up a data lake, which is a secure and centralized repository to hold data in its original form but prepared for analysis. A data lake breaks silos by combining different types of analytics, gaining better and deeper insights into the data.

Creating and managing a data lake is time-consuming and complicated because it involves extracting data from different sources, monitoring this data stream, collecting the keys on this data, defining transformations, etc.

The users can then utilize the centralized data catalog that holds the relevant data for analysis. Now that we know how these lakes are created most thoroughly with the help of Lake Formation let us conclude its benefits –

1. It helps build the data lakes in no time. With the help of the Lake Formation service, data can be moved, stored, cataloged, and set up in no time. All you need to provide to this service are the data sources and the security controls

required for this data. Lake Formation then crawls over this data and moves it to the newly created data lake on Amazon S3

2. Lake Formation service simplifies security management as per the security controls defined by the user. It leverages to define the governance and security policies centrally and then apply them to analyze the applications. These policies implement across the services without configuring them manually across other services, such as IAM, Key Management Service, etc. It eliminates the effort required in configuring the security policies across different services.

3. Lake Formation service enables the users to self-access the data stored in the lakes. The user creates the data catalog that holds data sets available to users and groups of users. It helps the users quickly find the right data for their specific needs. Records also ensure secured access to the data and make it easy for analysts to analyze it.

Predictive Analytics

To perform predictive analytics, AWS offers various machine learning services and tools to run on AWS data lakes.

- **Platform Services: Amazon SageMaker is a platform service offered by Amazon to build, train, and deploy machine learning models. It provides everything that is needed to connect to the training data, to select and** optimize the algorithms, and to deploy auto-scaling clusters of EC2.

- Application Services: For all those looking for a pre-built AI functionality in their applications, Amazon provides APIs for natural language processing. These services enable the developers to add an element of intelligence into their applications without building their models.

REVIEW QUESTIONS

Question 1

You are the solution architect for a national retail chain having stores in major cities. Each store uses an on-premise application for the sales transaction. At the end of the day at 11 pm, data from each store should upload to Amazon storage, which will be more than 30TB of data; the data then should be processed in Hadoop and the results stored in the data warehouse. What combination of AWS services will you use?

1.   Amazon Data Pipeline, Amazon S3, Amazon EMR, Amazon DynamoDB

2.   Amazon Data Pipeline, Amazon Elastic Block Storage, Amazon S3, Amazon EMR, Amazon Redshift

3.   Amazon Data Pipeline, Amazon S3, Amazon EMR, Amazon Redshift

4.   Amazon Data Pipeline, Amazon Kinesis, Amazon S3, Amazon
EMR, Amazon Redshift, Amazon EC2

Question 2

You are running a media-rich website with a global audience from us-east-1 for a customer in the publishing industry. The website updates every 20 minutes. The web-tier of the site sits on three EC2 instances inside an Auto Scaling Group. The Auto Scaling group configures to scale when CPU utilization of the cases is greater than 70%. The Auto Scaling group sits behind an Elastic Load Balancer. Your static content lives in S3 and is distributed globally by CloudFront. Your RDS database is already the largest instance size available. CloudWatch metrics show that your RDS instance usually has around 2GB of memory free and an average CPU utilization of 75%. Currently, it is taking your users in Japan and Australia approximately 3 - 5 seconds to load your website, and you have to ask to help reduce these load-times. How might you improve your page load times? [Select 3]

A) Setup CloudFront with dynamic content support to enable the caching of re-usable content from the media-rich website.

B) Set up a clone of your production environment in the Asia Pacific region and configure latency-based routing on Route 53.

C) Increase the Provisioned IOPS on the EBS Volume.

D) Change your Auto Scaling Group to scale when CPU Utilization is only 50%, rather than 70%.

E) Use ElastiCache to cache the most commonly accessed DB queries

Question 3

A customer has enabled website hosting on a bucket named "devtoolslogging" in the Singapore region. What website URL assigns to your bucket?

A) devtoolslogging.s3-website-ap-southeast-1.amazonaws.com

B) s3-website.devtoolslogging.amazonaws.com

C) s3-website.devtoolslogging.website-ap-southeast-1.amazonaws.com

D) devtoolslogging.ap-southeast-1.amazonaws.com

Question 4

A company does not want to manage their databases. Which of the following services altogethercontains databases provided by AWS?

A) AWS RDS

B) DynamoDB

C) Oracle RDS

D) Elastic Map Reduce

Question 5

Your company has recently migrated the on-premise application to AWS and deploying them in VPCs. As part of the proactive monitoring and audit purpose, they want to continuously analyze the Cloudtrail event logs to collect different operational metrics in real-time. For example:

- Total calls by IP, service, API call, IAM user

- Amazon EC2 API failures (or any other service)

- Anomalous behavior of Amazon EC2 API (or any other use)

- Top 10 API calls across all services

Which AWS services will you use?

1. S3, Kinesis Data Analytics, Lambda, DynamoDB

2. EC2, S3, Kinesis Data Analytics, DynamoDB

3. EC2, S3, Kinesis Data Analytics, Lambda, DynamoDB

4. Kinesis Data Firehose, S3, Kinesis Data Analytics, Lambda, DynamoDB

Question 6

Which of the following functions of the EMR HDFS file system?Choose 4.

1. It is a distributed, scalable, and portable file system for Hadoop.

2. It allows clusters to store data in Amazon S3.

3. Instance store and EBS volume storage area used for HDFS data.

4. Amazon EBS volumes attached to EMR clusters are ephemeral: the works delete upon set and instance termination.

5. HDFS is a common choice for persistent collections.

6. HDFS is a common choice for transient clusters.

Question 7

Which AWS service you will use for business analytics dashboards and visualizations?

1.   Amazon Athena

2.   Amazon EMR

3.   Amazon Elasticsearch Service

4.   Amazon QuickSight

Question 8

You have a database-style application that frequently has multiple reads and writes across the data set. Which of the following AWS storage services can host this application? [Select 2]

A) Elastic File Service (EFS)

B) Glacier

C) S3

D) EBS

Question 9

Which AWS database service will you choose for Online Analytical Processing (OLAP)?

1.   Amazon RDS

2.   Amazon Redshift

3.   Amazon Glacier

4.   Amazon DynamoDB

Question 10

Which of the following AWS services can you leverage to analyze logs for customer-facing applications and websites? Choose 2.

1.   Amazon S3

2.   Amazon Elasticsearch

3.   Amazon Athena

4.   Amazon Cloudwatch

Application Integration

Amazon SQS

SQS is a distributed message queuing system

- it allows you to decouple components of an application system, so they are independent.

- Ex: An EC2 Instance fails

- Another EC2 will pick it up, and

- The message will stay in the SQS queue.

- Pull based (not pushed)

- Standard Queues:

- Is the Default SQS setting

- Best effort ordering

- Message delivered at least once

- Visibility Timeout:

- The default is 30 seconds.

Amazon SNS

- Amazon SNS, Simple Notification Service, sends notifications from the Cloud.

- SNS is:

- Highly scalable

- Flexible

- Cost-effective

- Important in production systems
- SNS delivers messages to:
- Mobile devices
- SMS text
- Email
- SQS
- HTTP endpoints
- Trigger Lambda functions

AmazonSWF

Amazon Simple Workflow Service coordinates works across distributed application components

- SWF can run on:
- EC2 Instances
- Machines behind firewalls
- Amazon Cloud infrastructure
- SWF maximum retention period for a workflow is up to 1 year
- Always measured in seconds

REVIEW QUESTIONS

Question 1:

A company hosts a multiplayer game on AWS. The application uses Amazon EC2 instances in a single Availability Zone, and users connect over Layer 4. Solutions Architect has been tasked with making the architecture highly available and also more cost-effective.

How can the solutions architect best meet these requirements? (Select TWO)

1: Configure an Auto Scaling group to add or remove instances in the Availability Zone automatically

2: Increase the number of cases and use smaller EC2 instance types

3: Configure a Network Load Balancer in front of the EC2 instances

4: Configure an Application Load Balancer in front of the EC2 instances

5: Configure an Auto Scaling group to add or remove samples in multiple Availability Zones automatically

Question 2:

A solutions architect is designing the infrastructure to run an application on Amazon EC2 instances. The application requires high availability and must dynamically scale based on demand to be cost-efficient.

What should the solutions architect do to meet these requirements?

1: Configure an Application Load Balancer in front of an Auto Scaling group to deploy instances to multiple Regions

2: Configure an Amazon CloudFront distribution in front of an Auto Scaling group to deploy models to multiple Regions

3: Configure an Application Load Balancer in front of an Auto Scaling group to deploy instances to multiple Availability Zones

4: Configure an Amazon API Gateway API in front of an Auto Scaling group to deploy models to multiple Availability Zones

Question 3:

An application that runs a computational fluid dynamics workload uses a tightly-coupled HPC architecture that uses the MPI protocol and runs across many nodes. A service-managed deployment is required to minimize operational overhead.

Which deployment option is MOST suitable for provisioning and managing the resources required for this use case?

1: Use Amazon EC2 Auto Scaling to deploy instances in multiple subnets

2: Use AWS CloudFormation to deploy a Cluster Placement Group on EC2

3: Use AWS Batch to deploy a multi-node parallel job

4: Use AWS Elastic Beanstalk to provision and manage the EC2 instances

Question 4:

A security officer requires that access to company financial reports logs. The word stores in an Amazon S3 bucket. Additionally, any modifications to the log files must be detected.

Which actions should a solutions architect take?

1: Use S3 server access logging on the bucket that houses the reports with the read and write data events and the log file validation options enabled

2: Use S3 server access logging on the bucket that houses the pieces with the read and corresponds management events, and log file validation options enabled

3: Use AWS CloudTrail to create a new trail. Configure the path to log read and write data events on the S3 bucket that houses the reports. Log these events to a unique bucket, and enable log file validation

4: Use AWS CloudTrail to create a new trail. Configure the path to log read and write management events on the S3 bucket that houses the reports. Log these events to a unique bucket, and enable log file validation

Question 5:

An application runs on Amazon EC2 Linux instances. The application generates log files that write using standard API calls. A storage solution requires that it can be used to store the files indefinitely and must allow concurrent access to all files.

Which storage service meets these requirements, and is the MOST cost-effective?

1: Amazon EBS

2: Amazon EFS

3: Amazon EC2 instance store

4: Amazon S3

Question 6:

A company has some statistical data stored in an Amazon RDS database. The company wants to allow users to access this information using an API. A solutions architect must create a solution that helps sporadic access to the data, ranging from no requests to large bursts of traffic.

Which solution should the solutions architect suggest?

1: Set up an Amazon API Gateway and use Amazon ECS

2: Set up an Amazon API Gateway and use AWS Elastic Beanstalk

3: Set up an Amazon API Gateway and use AWS Lambda functions

4: Set up an Amazon API Gateway and use Amazon EC2 with Auto Scaling

Question 7:

A web application in a three-tier architecture runs on a fleet of Amazon EC2 instances. Performance issues reports and investigations point to insufficient swap space. The operations team requires monitoring to determine if this is correct.

What should a solutions architect recommend?

1: Configure an Amazon CloudWatch SwapUsage metric dimension. Monitor the SwapUsage extent in the EC2 metrics in CloudWatch

2: Use EC2 metadata to collect information, then publish it to Amazon CloudWatch custom metrics. Monitor SwapUsage metrics in CloudWatch

3: Install an Amazon CloudWatch agent on the instances. Run an appropriate script on a set schedule. Monitor SwapUtilization metrics in CloudWatch

4: Enable detailed monitoring in the EC2 console. Create an Amazon CloudWatch SwapUtilization custom metric. Monitor SwapUtilization metrics in CloudWatch

Question 8:

A gaming company collects real-time data and stores it in an on-premises database system. The company is migrating to AWS and needs better performance for the database. A solutions architect has asked to recommend an in-memory database that supports data replication.

Which database should a solutions architect recommend?

1: Amazon RDS for MySQL

2: Amazon RDS for PostgreSQL

3: Amazon ElastiCache for Redis

4: Amazon ElastiCache for Memcached

Question 9:

To increase performance and redundancy for an application, a company has decided to run multiple implementations in different AWS Regions behind network load balancers. The company currently advertises the application using two public IP addresses from separate /24 address ranges and would prefer not to change these.

Which actions should a solutions architect take? (Select TWO)

1: Create an Amazon Route 53 geolocation-based routing policy

2: Create an AWS Global Accelerator and attach endpoints in each AWS Region

3: Assign new static anycast IP addresses and modify any existing pointers

4: Migrate both public IP addresses to the AWS Global Accelerator

5: Create PTR records to map currentlyavailable IP addresses to an Alias

Question 10:

A highly elastic application consists of three tiers. The application tier runs in an Auto Scaling group and processes data and writes it to an Amazon RDS MySQL database. The Solutions Architect wants to restrict access to the database tier to accept traffic from the instances in the application tier.

How can the Solutions Architect configure secure access to the database tier?

1: Configure the database security group to allow traffic only from the application security group

2: Configure the database security group to allow traffic only from port 3306

3: Configure a Network ACL on the database subnet to deny all traffic to ports other than 3306

4: Configure a Network ACL on the database subnet to allow all traffic from the application subnet

Question 11:

A website runs on a Microsoft Windows server in an on-premises data center. The web server is being migrated to Amazon EC2 Windows instances in multiple Availability Zones on AWS. The web server currently uses data stored in on-premises network-attached storage (NAS) device.

Which replacement to the NAS file share is MOST resilient and durable?

1: Migrate the file share to Amazon EBS

2: Migrate the file share to AWS Storage Gateway

3: Migrate the file share to Amazon FSx for Windows File Server

4: Migrate the file share to Amazon Elastic File System (Amazon EFS)

Question 12:

An application monitored using Amazon GuardDuty. A Solutions Architect needs to be notified by email of medium to high severity events. How can this be achieved?

1: Configure an Amazon CloudWatch alarm that triggers based on a GuardDuty metric

2: Create an Amazon CloudWatch Events rule that triggers an Amazon SNS topic

3: Create an Amazon CloudWatch Logs rule that triggers an AWS Lambda function

4: Configure an Amazon CloudTrail alarm the triggers based on GuardDuty API activity

Question 13:

A solutions architect is creating a document submission application for a school. The application will use an Amazon S3 bucket for storage. The solution must prevent the accidental deletion of the documents and ensure that all versions of the papers are available. Users must be able to upload and modify the copies.

Which combination of actions should it take to meet these requirements? (Select TWO)

1: Set read-only permissions on the bucket

2: Enable versioning on the bucket

3: Attach an IAM policy to the bucket

4: Enable MFA Delete on the bucket

5: Encrypt the bucket using AWS SSE-S3

Question 14:

An HR application stores employment records on Amazon S3. Regulations mandate the forms retains for seven years. Once created, the records are accessed infrequently for the first three months and then must be available within 10 minutes if required after that.

Which lifecycle action meets the requirements while MINIMIZING cost?

1: Store the data in S3 Standard for three months, then transition to S3 Glacier

2: Store the data in S3 Standard-IA for three months, then transition to S3 Glacier

3: Store the data in S3 Standard for three months, then transition to S3 Standard-IA

4: Store the data in S3 Intelligent Tiering for three months, then transition to S3 Standard-IA

Question 15:

An application calls to a REST API running on Amazon EC2 instances behind an Application Load Balancer (ALB). Most API calls complete quickly. What steps can a Solutions Architect take to minimize the effects of the long-running API calls?

1: Change the EC2 instance to one with enhanced networking to reduce latency

2: Create an Amazon SQS queue and decouple the long-running API calls

3: Increase the ALB idle timeout to allow the long-running requests to complete

4: Change the ALB to a Network Load Balancer (NLB) and use SSL/TLS termination

Question 16:

A company is deploying an Amazon ElastiCache for Redis cluster. Enhance security, and a password should be required to access the database. What should the solutions architect use?

1: AWS Directory Service

2: AWS IAM Policy

3: Redis AUTH command

4: VPC Security Group

AWS Security, Identity & Compliance

General Security practices are essential from an architect's perspective for the exam.

AWS CloudTrail

It is an essential service from a security perspective. The AWS CloudTrail service can use to monitor all API activity from the AWS account. Whether you are issuing API calls either from the SDK or PowerShell or using the console, everything will record in the AWS CloudTrail service.

· It's also perfect when you want to ensure compliance for your company.

· Also, if you suspect any malicious activity in your account, you can check the CloudTrail logs to see if any irregular API activities have fires. Some resources span up, which is not supposed to create; you can see for this API calls in the CloudTrail logs.

· As an architect, you should always enable CloudTrail logs for all regions. It also ensures that if any future parts get created by AWS, they automatically get covered.

IAM

When you are creating IAM users, ensure to give them access based on 'least privilege.' In other words, ensure that you give them permissions based on only the tasks they are going to do.

· Use multi-factor authentication wherever possible.

· Change the password policy; don't keep the default password policy. In the past system, you can mention the characters to be specified when creating the password and how long the password should last (the password).

· Disable the root access keys.

Buckets in S3

For the buckets in S3, you have the bucket policy, which can use to manage the access via the underlying objects. Even when you're giving access to external AWS accounts, remember that you can do this via the bucket policy.

The pre-signed URLs enables you to give a time limit for when a user can access an object.

IAM Roles

IAM roles use for secure access to your resources. Let's say you have an application on an EC2 instance that needs to access a service like S3 or DynamoDB and attach an IAM Role to that instance with the specific privilege.

It' so use access keys, but w during development time, when you go onto deployment or production, ensure that you use IAM Roles for secure access.

Even if you are using a lambda function to access an external resource like DynamoDB or S3, ensure that an IAM Role is attached to the lambda function.

Network Security

If you want an instance in a private subnet to access public resources like DynamoDB, S3, or KMS, remember you can't use the NAT gateway. You then have to use a unique feature known as VPC Endpoints.

There are two types of VPC Endpoints:

VPC Gateway Endpoints: This uses when you want to access either S3 or DynamoDB.

VPC Interface Endpoint: This uses when you want to access other services such as KMS.

What you do is that you create a VPC endpoint to your service, attach it to the VPC, and then you can make your instance in the private subnet access that resource via the endpoint.

For Redshift, if you want the data during the LOAD or COPY process to be private (that is, it should not go via the internet) via a VPC, you can enable one feature known as Redshift Enhance VPC Routing. If you want to monitor IP addresses of traffic into your VPC, use VPC Flow Logs.

Use Bastion host if an administrator needs to administer instances in your private subnet. The bastion host will kill in the public subnet; ensure the right security groups are in place only to allow access to the administrator's workstation.

REVIEW QUESTIONS

Question 1

Amazon Cognito means ....

Question 2:

When applying the security best practices, how should your team members access resources in the AWS account?

Question 3:

What should AWS do to prevent customers from using an unsustainable part of available resources?

Question 4:

How can you describe the cloud service model known as infrastructure as a service?

Question 5:

What method of authentication would you need to access your files remotely using the CLI?

Question 6:

What description can you give the method of protecting your data locally on-site, in transit, and during storage on the AWS cloud platform?

Question 7:

What is the full file size allowed in Amazon S3?

1.   5 terabytes

2.   0 bytes

3.   5 gigabytes

4.   Unlimited

Question 8:

What is the significant advantage of using resource tags with your assets on Amazon Web Services?

Question 9:

An application running on an Amazon ECS container instance using the EC2 launch type needs permission to write data to Amazon DynamoDB.

How can you assign these permissions only to the specific ECS task that is running the application?

1: Create an IAM policy with permissions to DynamoDB and attach it to the container instance

2: Create an IAM policy with permissions to DynamoDB and assign It to a task using the taskRoleArn parameter

3: Use a security group to allow outbound connections to DynamoDB and give it to the container instance

4: Modify the AmazonECSTaskExecutionRolePolicy policy to add permissions for DynamoDB

Question 10:

The solution architect is designing a new workload, in which AWS Lambda functions will access Amazon DynamoDB tables.

What are the MOST secure means of granting the Lambda function access to the DynamoDB table?

1: Create an identity and access management (IAM) role with the required permissions to access DynamoDB tables, and assign parts to Lambda functions

2: Create a DynamoDB username and password and give them to the Developer to use in the Lambda function

3: Create an identity and access management (IAM) role allowing access from AWS Lambda and assign the part to the DynamoDB table

Network Architectures

These objectives are selecting high-performing network solutions and designing cost-optimized network architectures for your workload. You can get some questions on the use case scenario of high-performing networking solutions in the exam, so you need to understand these concepts in detail. Let's try to figure out what could ask in the examination.

When considering Network Architectures, there are three types of network solutions for your workload. They are flat network architectures, segmented network architectures, and hybrid connectivity. Let's discuss flat network architectures first. So, in the flat network architecture, you have a single VPC architecture, which means a single account in an available VPC. Itis how Virtual Private Cloud develops; you select a CIDR for a VPC and split it into subnets and individual availability zones. Then the subnets are placed into routing tables where they subdivide into Public and Private Subnets. You can have five CIDR blocks attached to one VPC.

So in single VPC architecture, limited data transfer is considered unless you have dependencies that reach AZ boundaries. You can even have more than 300,000 IP addresses so your workloads can start to scale. And you can also split native constructs into Subnets Route Tables, NACLs, and Security Groups. So if you have a VPC architecture in which you can have several hyper-scale customers who can operate hundreds of thousands of services like microservices within a single account in an available VPC, then the network architecture suitable for you is single VPC architecture.

Let's say you have a single VPC that's Multi-Tenant, and then you need to ensure that one of these tenants does not consume all your resources and not sharing with other users. So it can get rather challenging to have everyone in the same bucket when you talk of cost allocation or policy enforcement. Thus, VPC Sharing is the ideal approach to use a single VPC with multiple accounts. It uses the Amazon Resource Access Manager to share your subnets and resources with other charges in your AWS organization like the Transit Gateway, Route 53, and Resolving Rules within your VPC.

So in the single VPC multiple accounts or shared VPC model, you share a subnet to participants. Then they may launch their resources like EC2 instances or databases or ELBs within these subnets that you own. It is essential from the exam perspective. VPC sharing has account-specific cost allocation, a single VPC blast radius, and shared DNS. Still, there is limited access control for application owners. Policy control and isolation that the individual AWS account provides can implement on that the single VPC layer. This method of centralizing and reusing VPC components reduce costs for the management and maintenance of your environment.

Ideally, when users look at these designs, they seek to optimize the costs. That's why they place them into one single VPC because they have a lot of dependencies between workloads. Thus, users don't require mediums like the Transit Gateway, VPC peering, and private link for the VPC management with one single VPC. Let's move onto the segmented network architecture.

In Segmented network architecture, we have multiple accounts in multiple VPCs. So, this architecture prefers for large companies that can control and push beyond the AWS account limits. So this architecture is required when users want isolation between their dev tests and production workloads or want to isolate their business unit and workload category.

And another reason that it designs to isolate the individual microservices completely. For example, if you have a PCI or HIPAA compliance workload, then you can use it, or to simply separate the software testing and production environments. You can also isolate your blast radius if your workload crosses the VPC and the account boundaries. It provides you with the distributed service limitations that you can use to scale on AWS.

This approach increases the complexity of IP management, like what type of IP range or CIDR do I assign for a bunch of my VPCs? How can I communicate with lots of other VPCs? You also need to consider how you handle access control between resources across different VPCs and IAM and networking accounts.

So here come several patterns of VPC networking connectivity. First, we have VPC Peering. Let's say you wanted to connect all your VPCs. In this case, you use VPC Peering to create a complete communication network between the VPCs. VPC Peering is easy to set up and has no bandwidth limitations. VPC Peering can enable for VPCs between the same regions, across regions, or between different accounts. But, let's say you have four VPCs, so you need to set up six peering links with the four VPCs and approve and configure routing for each of them. It could ask in the examination.

If you want to manage multiple networks and infrastructures, you can use Transit Gateway for that purpose. When you have hundreds of VPCs and connections, Transit Gateway eliminates the time-consuming process of linking individual VPCs with each other through VPC peering and creating VPN tunnels between the on-premise and each VPC to allow on-premise connectivity. It uses either a VPN connection or Direct Connect connection. It's like you try to merge your edge connectivity with AWS. By default, it can scale up to 5,000 VPCs and supports equal-cost multi-path VPNs.

Moreover, it also allows you to route flexibly and provides you with multiple routing tables. You must understand the difference between VPC peering and Transit Gateway from an exam perspective.Let's see the concept of PrivateLink, which is very important for the exam. Now every application needs to communicate with one another through three-way TCP handshakes. So PrivateLink is specially built for traditional TCP client-server relation where you have a client on one side. A server lives in a different VPC. You create a hole in another VPC to provide services on a specific port and an IP address to another VPC.It is different from the VPC Peering and Transit Gateway since it punishes a hole for that service. It does not provide two-way connectivity for the entire VPC's. It uses because it entirely reduces the visibility to and from shared services.

It also supports IAM policy on the endpoint itself, and it solves large and complex network address translation.

Let's consider a use case in which you use PrivateLink to access dependencies on-premise with overlapping IPs. In this architecture, you have on-premise services, and you have cloud-based services and want to share these resources. One option is to use a mediator or NAT VPC in this model because it allows you to set up bi-directional private links to expose endpoints in the cloud and on-premise. These are a virtual interface that you are not targeting, like a single server or a load balancer on-prem.

Therefore, the IP address of your client in the VPC is 10.0.1.15, and your local server has the same IP address. Therefore, here you put PrivateLink into the client's VPC. You have a network load balancer in the mediator or NAT VPC. Its IP target passes to the local database server through a direct connection... When the server receives the request, the request comes from the IP address of the mediator.

The reverse is that I have a private link in the mediator or NAT VPC, and I expose my service via a personalconnection in the NLB within the VPC itself. The same IP addresses of the client-server solve the NAT issue, as I mentioned earlier. You can see the difference in the diagram below:

Now how can you use PrivateLink for cost optimization? Thus, Centralizing interface VPC endpoint is one of the best ways of deploying PrivateLink to optimize costs. Some customers choose to host private

229

link endpoints in shared services VPC because it reduces the cost of AWS PrivateLink endpoints based on the traffic profile. But you may end up paying for the data transfer costs when you have a Kinesis endpoint or something that uses a lot of bandwidth. Then you would just host the endpoint yourself.

Another thing to consider in this situation is when you create a PrivateLink; the service creates a private hosted zone for you. The PrivateLink service owns this personal hosted zone. You don't own it, so you can't connect it to other VPCs. Therefore, the privately hosted endpoints outside the VPC cannot be attached. Data processing costs can also increase according to how consumers communicate with a centralized endpoint. Thus, if you want to reduce costs and private link endpoints, that might be a good option for you.

Now, let's see the hybrid connectivity models that you need to know generally for the exam. First is AWS Site-to-Site VPN connectivity. The first option is to terminate the site-to-site VPN connection on a Transit Gateway. And then, Transit Gateway spreads connectivity to thousands of VPCs. The second model involves completing your Site-to-Site VPN connection on a Virtual Private Gateway attached to a single VPC. The third option is to terminate the VPN on an EC2 instance that runs VPN software from the AWS marketplace. You should choose to use the Transit Gateway for your VPN termination because it simplifies management by reducing the number of VPN tunnels and BGP sessions to handle. And it also scales horizontally in terms of throughput and the scale of the number of VPCs.

While VPN is an excellent option to start up, but may not be ideal for some production traffic. Therefore, choose AWS direct connect, which gives high bandwidth connectivity between your data center and the AWS. It is all from hybrid connectivity that could ask in the examination.

Let's discuss some of the differences between AWS Global Accelerator and CloudFront, which is very important from the exam perspective. Both offer you the AWS backbone network to decrease latency for end-users. So if you have a website that is deployed just to one region, use CloudFront. It will also give you the capability of Response Caching and Lambda Edges. In Response Caching, you can cache static assets or full pages of your website close to end-users, which is very handy. And Lambda edge allows you to execute small pieces of software in a region close to the user in edge location. Due to this reason, CloudFront is a better option for minimizing latency for end-users. Still, then, Global Accelerator offers you two public IPs, and because of that, it can work with any DNS system.

And in terms of failover between regions, the global accelerator is best because it offers you Multi-region failover. So, in case your website is deployed in more than one area. It's good to use CloudFront and Global Accelerator to deliver content to end-users and split traffic between sites.

In case you use API, which would never need caching, then a global accelerator is aright choice because caching is not required. Global accelerators can distribute content and distribute API responses to end-users, and also, it can switch traffic between regions. It also distributes traffic between multiple areas. Another feature of Global Accelerator is that its IP addressresolves regionally.

Conclusion

Amazon continues to roll out new regional places, so you're most likely to have access to a neighboring service location and the abundant AWS ecosystem.

AWS Is the Leading Cloud-Computing Provider. AWS is exceptionally popular. However, its popularity has the impact of making the service much better. Today, Amazon has an enhancing cycle taking place:

- Having more users produces a higher volume of usage, which increases the amount of hardware Amazon purchases, which reduces its costs utilizing economies of scale, which hands down to users in the type of lower prices.

-Because of the large number of users, companies that use complimentary services (online application integration, for example) decide to initially put their services in AWS, making the total service much better, which draws in more users.

Everywhere you turn, the word development is a hot subject. Individuals acknowledge that innovation makes life much better and can improve the future for generations to come.

AWS has changed how technology provides to clients and, as a result, has enabled a surge of development. The development and low cost related to AWS permit little and big businesses to rapidly and cheaply introduce brand-new offerings as one development consultant put it:

AWS has decreased the cost of failure. AWS lets you quickly check out a brand-new item to see whether it "gets traction." Moreover, if a new offering gets traction and starts to accelerate, AWS lets you quickly scale it. On the other hand, if the service does not attain adoption, that's no issue-- the ease of shutting down AWS resources means that very little is lost if an ingenious perspective offering does not turn out.".

I forecast that a lot more innovation will happen as more individuals and companies become knowledgeable about AWS and its capabilities. AWS will be to the details.

AWS Is Cost Effective.

Much of that expense reduction is because of AWS: its on-demand low prices and simple termination without any charges make it possible to utilize and spend precisely as much computing capacity as you require when you require it.

The expense effectiveness of AWS isn't limited to start-ups, though. Every company can take advantage of access to inexpensive computing that doesn't need a prolonged commitment. It's a sign of the significantbenefits of AWS that much.

When there, the existing supplier community is terrified of what will occur.

Customers begin to demand AWS-like prices and benefit from them.

Amazon is a different company. Unlike many companies that strive to raise their own earnings margins, Amazon passes on the advantages of energy at lower costs. There's no factor to anticipate that this method will change.

Amazon can make your IT dollars go further if you're a part of any company, little or big. It's substantially more expense significant than the conventional mode of acquiring IT resources: large up-front payments with little certainty about whether the amount provisioned is too small (or too much).

AWS Aligns Your Organization.

In the 1980s, the increase of networked PCs (the client-server architecture) transformed mainframes into a traditional environment-- and led to Microsoft ending up being the dominant gamer in the software market. In the 1990s, the Internet made the Web (and HTTP process) the de facto architecture for all applications-and, led to the domination of businesses such as Google and, of course, Amazon.Cloud computing is the next-generation platform for computing. Its characteristics of highly scalable, on-demand computing services that are readily available within minutes and bring no requirement for long-lasting dedication will end up being the foundation for all future applications. As the saying goes, resistance is futile.

Its record of innovation and rate competitiveness is unrivaled in the market. I forecast that ten years from now, AWS will be the Microsoft or Google of its period. Your organization should become knowledgeable about AWS and determine how to utilize it successfully-- otherwise. It may discover the IT equivalent of a buggy whip maker after Henry Ford developed the assembly line.

AWS Is Good for Your Career.

The great business is to be the best individual at the right time and in the best place. To be the best person is all you have-your ability to work, productive working relationships, and wisdom. No matter which field or function you operate, these attributes will help you succeed.

However, remaining in the ideal place at the perfect time has a lot to do with insight about where a brand-new market, made possible by some development, is emerging and planting your flag there.

In the 1920s, or entered TV services in the 1950s, or the Internet in the 1990s, as new markets sought expertise to build great companies, people entering the automotive industry experienced tremendous opportunities.

Technology innovation produces powerful abilities gaps in the market and makes those with understanding and experience necessary. Suppose you think that AWS is. The next-generation platform, too, can represent "the best place at the time" for you.

Answers to Review Questions

Computer Answers

Question 1 Answer: 1

One is correct. The best way to achieve this is to use an event notification on the S3 bucket that triggers a function that runs the code.

Twoare incorrect. Lambda does not poll S3.

Three is incorrect. You would not use Amazon SNS in this scenario as it is an unnecessary additional step.

Question 2 Answer(s): 3

One is incorrect. EFS is a file-based storage system that is accessed using the NFS protocol.

Twoare incorrect. EBS is a block-based storage system for mounting volumes.

Three is correct. Amazon S3 is an object-based storage system that uses standards-based REST web interfaces to work with objects.

Fourare incorrect. Amazon FSx for Windows File Server provides a fully managed Microsoft filesystem that is mounted using SMB.

Question 3 Answer(s): 4

One is incorrect. Reserved instances require a commitment over 1 or 3 years.

Twoare incorrect. Spot instances are suitable for cost-sensitive workloads that can afford to be interrupted. This workload must complete, so Spot instances would not be ideal.

Three is incorrect. Dedicated Instances are Amazon EC2 instances that run in a VPC on hardware dedicated to a single customer. It would be more expensive, and there is no need for dedicated hardware in this case.

Fourare correct. On-demand instances are ideal for short-term or unpredictable workloads. You don't get a discount, but you do have more flexibility with no commitments.

Question 4 Answer(s): 2

One is incorrect. You cannot nest buckets (create buckets inside other buckets).

Two is correct. You can mimic the hierarchy of a filesystem by creating a folder in your buckets.

Three is incorrect. You cannot upload objects within other objects.

Fourare incorrect. Tiering your data is done for performance, not to mimic a filesystem.

Question 5 Answer(s): 4

One is incorrect. Aurora Global Database spans multiple regions for disaster recovery.

Twoare incorrect. Aurora Replicas scales read operations but do not allow writes to multiple DB instances.

Three is incorrect. Aurora Cross-Region Replicase scale read operations across regions. They do not allow writes to DB instances in multiple AZs.

Fourare correct. Amazon Aurora Multi-Master adds the ability to scale out write performance across multiple Availability Zones and provides configurable read after write consistency.

Question 6 Answer(s): 1

One is correct. DynamoDB is a schema-less NoSQL database that provides push-button scaling.

Twoare incorrect. ElastiCache is an in-memory relational database, so it is not schema-less.

Three is incorrect. Amazon RDS is a relational database (not schema-less) and uses EC2 instancesnot to offer push-button scaling.

Fourare incorrect. Amazon Aurora is a relational database (not schema-less) and uses EC2 instances not to offer push-button scaling.

Question 7 Answer(s): 3

One is incorrect. DynamoDB Global Tables provides a multi-region, multi-master database solution.

Twoare incorrect. DynamoDB Auto Scaling is for scaling read and write capacity.

Three is correct. DynamoDB Streams maintains a list of item level changes and can integrate with Lambda to create triggers.

Fourare incorrect. DynamoDB DAX provides microsecond latency for reading requests to DynamoDB tables.

Question 8 Answer(s):2

One is incorrect. RedShift is not a schema-less database; it is a relational database.

Two is correct. RedShift is a data warehouse optimized for online analytics processing (OLAP).

Three is incorrect. RedShift optimizes online analytics processing (OLAP) use cases, not online transactional processing (OLTP) use cases.

Fourare incorrect. RedShift can be analyzed using SQL, not Hadoop (should use EMR).

Question 9 Answer(s): 1

One is correct. Redis provides data persistence.

Twoare incorrect. Memcached does not provide data persistence.

Question 10 Answer(s): 4

One is incorrect. You do not attach Internet gateways to subnets.

Twoare incorrect. You do not attach Internet gateways to subnets.

Three is incorrect. You do not attach Internet gateways to AZs.

Fourare correct. Internet Gateways are attached to the VPC.

Question 11 Answer(s): 2

One is incorrect. VPCs are not global.

Two is correct. VPC is regional and can create a VPC in each region.

Three is incorrect. An availability zone exists within a region, and a VPC can span subnets attached to all AZs in the area.

Question 12 Answer(s): 4

One is incorrect. An MX record is a mail exchange record for email servers.

Twoare incorrect. A record simply points a name to an IP address.

Three is incorrect. A CNAME record cannot points at a domain apex record like dctlabs.com.

Fourare correct. An Alias record can be used with domain apex records and can point to an ELB.

Question 13 Answer(s): 1

One is correct. The ALB only supports layer seven, which is HTTP and HTTPS – not TCP.

Twoare incorrect. This is the correct combination of listener/protocol.

Three is incorrect. This is the correct combination of listener/protocol.

Question 14 Answer(s):2

One is incorrect. EC2 Auto Scaling is not an example of vertical scaling.

Two is correct. EC2 Auto Scaling scales horizontally by launching or terminating EC2 instances.

Question 15 Answer(s):3

One is incorrect. AWS Managed VPN uses the public Internet, so it's not considered a private connection or low-latency.

Twoare incorrect. AWS VPN CloudHub uses for creating a hub and spoke topology of VPN connections. Use the public Internet, not personal relationships.

Three is correct. AWS Direct Connect uses private network connections into the AWS Cloud and is high-bandwidth and low-latency. It is suitable for establishing hybrid cloud configurations.

Fourare incorrect. A Transit VPC uses for connecting VPCs across regions.

Question 16 Answer(s):3

One is incorrect. Route 53 latency based routing does not provide automatic failover or 2 IP addresses.

Twoare incorrect. Amazon CloudFront is a content delivery network. It does not perform automatic routing across regions and doesn't provide 2 IP addresses for whitelisting.

Three is correct. AWS Global Accelerator provides static IP addresses that act as a fixed entry point to application endpoints in a single or multiple AWS Regions. It uses two static anycast IP addresses.

Fourare incorrect. Route 53 geolocation-based routing does not provide automatic failover or 2 IP addresses.

Question 16 Answer(s):2

One is incorrect. AWS Lambda does not use as the public endpoint for API Gateway.

Twois correct. Amazon CloudFront does use as the public endpoint for API Gateway.

Three is incorrect. Amazon S3 does not use the public endpoint for API Gateway.

Fourare incorrect. Amazon ECS does not use as the public endpoint for API Gateway.

Question 17 Answer(s):3

One is incorrect. To provide low-latency access with Amazon S3, you would need to copy the videos to buckets in different regions worldwide and then create a mechanism for directing employees to the local copy.

Twoare incorrect. AWS Global Accelerator uses for directing users of applications to local points of presence around the world. It does not operate for accessing the content in S3. It does use with ELB and EC2.

Three is correct. CloudFront is a content delivery network and is ideal for this use case. It caches the content around the world, provides a single endpoint address, and uses a single source for the videos.

Fourare incorrect. AWS Lambda is a compute service and not suited to this use case.

243

Storage Answers

Question 1 Answer:

B. Amazon DynamoDB

Question 2 Answers:

A.   Memcached

D.   Redis

Question 3Answers:

A.   Creating an Amazon S3 bucket

D.   Configuring a VPC security group

E.   Creating an Oracle RDS database

Question 4 Answer: C

The AWS Documentation mentions the below Linux Amazon Machine Images use one of two types of virtualization: paravirtual (PV) or hardware virtual machine (HVM). The main difference between PV and HVM AMIs is how they boot and whether they can take advantage of unique hardware extensions (CPU, network, and storage) for better performance.

Question 5 Answer:

B.   Launch configuration

Question 6 Answer:

D. Enforces a minimum number of running Amazon EC2 instances.

E. Responds to changing conditions by adding or terminating Amazon EC2 instances.

F. Launches instances from a specified Amazon Machine Image (AMI).

Question 7 Answers:

C. Store the file in S3 Standard

Question 8 Answers:

A. For files older than 30 days, create lifecycle rules to move these files to Amazon S3 Standard Infrequent Access and use Amazon Glacier to move files older than 40 days.

[Question 9 Answers:

D. EBS Throughput Optimized HDD (st1)

Networking Answers

Question 1 Answer:A,D

A 500% increase is beyond the scope of a well-designed single server system to absorb unless it is already hugely overspecialized to accommodate this sort of burst load. An AWS solution for this situation might include S3 static web pages with client-side scripting to meet the high demand for information pages. Also, using a NoSQL database to collect customer registration for asynchronous processing and SQS backed by scalable compute to keep up with the requests. LightSail does provide a scalable provisioned service solution. However, these still need to be designed and planned by you and offer no significant advantage in this situation. A standby server is a good idea but will not help with the anticipated 500x load increase.

Question 2 Answer: A

Cognito will handle the user authentication; Lambda provides the serverless architecture that allows you to run your code without deploying it in an EC2 instance. Finally, S3 provides scalable object storage.

Question 3 Answer: D

The lease of an instance can only be changed between the "dedicated" lease hosting variants. It cannot change from the default rental hosting to the default rental hosting.

Question 4 Answer(s): A,C,D

Route 53 has the following routing strategies-simple, weighted, delayed, failover, multi-value response, and geographic location. And location

Question 5 Answer: B

Please note that if the data is in the same area, there will be no charge for transferring the data from EC2 to S3. AWS solution architects must know.

Question 6 Answer: B,D

CSV, YAML, XML, and JSON are all data formats (rather than languages). Still, only JSON and YAML can be used to create CloudFormation templates.

Question 7 Answer: C

The NACL's can be modified to be most secure by only denying the traffic from IP addresses.

Question 8 Answer: B

At present, the S3 category is; standard, standard infrequent access, an area infrequently accessed, reduced redundant storage, and Glacier & Glacier Deep Archive for archiving. Thin redundant storage is the only S3 category that does not provide 99.999999999% durability. Therefore, any answer that includes narrow redundant storage is incorrect.

Question 9 Answer: C, D

You should consider raising the bids of task nodes so that your nodes will not terminate, and even consider converting task nodes into on-demand instances to ensure that they are not released prematurely.

Question 10 Answer: A, B, C

The correct answers are Enterprise, Business, Developer, and the Basic free level. Remember that Free Tier is a Billing rebate, not an account or support level.

Question 11 Answer: A,D

All data transferred between any type of gateway appliance and AWS storage is encrypted using SSL. By default, all data stored by AWS Storage Gateway in S3 is encrypted server-side with Amazon S3-Managed Encryption Keys (SSE-S3). Also, when using the file gateway, you can optionally configure each file share to have your objects encrypted with AWS KMS-Managed Keys using SSE-KMS.

Question 12 Answer: B,E

Network throughput is the apparent bottleneck. In this question, it will not tell you whether the proxy server is in a public subnet or a private subnet.

If it is in a public subnet, the size of the proxy server instance may not be large enough to handle its throughput. If the proxy server is in a private subnet, it must use a NAT instance or NAT gateway to communicate with the Internet. If it is a NAT instance, it may also be under-configured in terms of size. Therefore, you should increase the size of the proxy server and NAT solution.

Question 13 Answer: B, C,D

EBS, S3, and EFS all allow the user to configure encryption at rest using either the AWS Key Management Service (KMS) or, in some cases, using customer-provided keys. The exception on the list is ElastiCache for Memcached, which does not offer a native encryption service, although ElastiCache for Redis does.

Question 14 Answers: C,D

Trying to use S3 without File Gateway in front would be a significant impact on the user environment. Using File Gateway is the recommended way to use S3 with shared document pools. Life-cycle management and Infrequent Access storage are available for both S3 and EFS. A restriction, however, is that 'Using Amazon EFS with Microsoft Windows is not supported.' File Gateway does not support iSCSI on the client-side.

Question 15 Answers: C

Increasing the size increases both network throughput and compute power.

Content Delivery Answers

Question 1 Answer: A, B, D

Signed URLs and signed cookies are two ways to ensure that users can be authorized when they try to access files in an S3 bucket. One approach generates URLs, while the other creates unique cookies. Still, both require an application and policy to make to develop and manage these items.

Question 2 Answer: E

The Cloud Adoption Framework concentrates on the early stages of cloud adoption. Any reinvention of the business process is therefore not inherently considered as part of CAF.

Question 3 Answer: B

Amazon CloudFront has two types of distribution Web and RTMP. The limit of web distribution per account is 200, and RTMP per account is 100.

Question 4 Answer: B

Geo-restriction means you can restrict your content access in countries where you do not want to show your content. You can blacklist all countries you want to limit your scope, or you can whitelist the states for which you want to allow access to your content.

Question 5 Answer: A

Amazon CloudFront can work as an origin server or non-origin server. As an origin server, it includes Amazon EC2, Amazon S3 bucket, and Elastic Loud balancing or Route 53. As a non-origin server, it contains on-premises web servers.

Question 6 Answer: C

Through an invalidation API, you can remove malicious or harmful objects before their expiration time from all edge locations. That is an invalidation request.

Question 7 Answer: A

With CloudFront, you can use HTTP or HTTPS. Still, if you want to use SSL, then you need to use a default CloudFront URL that creates during the creation of distribution, or you can create a customized URL with your SSL certificate. There are two separate ways to do Custom SSL depending on budget and outdated browser.

- Dedicated IP Custom SSL

- SNI (Server Name Identification) Custom SSL

Question 8 Answer: A

CloudFront supports GET, POST, HEAD, PUT, PATCH, DELETE, and OPTIONS HTTP requests. PUT, POST, PATCH, and DELETE bids, responses are not cached in CloudFront.

Question 9 Answer: D

Amazon Route 53, a DNS Web service, is scalable, highly available, and a cost-effective medium to direct the visitors to a website, a virtual server, or a load balancer.

Question 10 Answers:

You can use the Subnet Association tab to associate or disassociate subnets to the selected AWS Route Table.

Databases Answers

Question 1 Answer: B

Add multi-factor authentication (MFA) with a Cognito user pool is the correct answer.

Add multi-factor authentication (MFA) with a Cognito user pool is the solution that needs to implements to add the extra layer of security.

Question 2 Answer: D

AWS Certificate Manager is the correct answer. AWS Certificate Manager (ACM) makes it easy to provision, manage, and deploy SSL/TLS certificates on AWS managed resources.

Question 3 Answer: B

Traffic mirroring is the correct answer.

Traffic mirroring copies network traffic from an elastic network interface of an Amazon EC2 instance, and then you can then send the traffic to out-of-band security and monitoring appliances.

Question 4 Answer: D,E

Redis and Memcached are the two cache engines available in Elasticache.

Question 5 Answer:A

Rule: 100, Type: HTTP, Protocol: TCP, Port range: 80, Source: 0.0.0.0/0, Allow/Deny: ALLOW is the correct answer.

1) Rule: 100, Type: HTTP, Protocol: TCP, Port range: 443, Source: 0.0.0.0/0, Allow/Deny: ALLOW is incorrect because it uses the port 443, which is the HTTPS port

2) Rule: 100, Type: HTTP, Protocol: TCP, Port range: 53, Source: 0.0.0.0/0, Allow/Deny: ALLOW is incorrect because it uses the port 53, which is the DNS port

3) Rule: 100, Type: HTTP, Protocol: TCP, Port range: 22, Source: 0.0.0.0/0, Allow/Deny: ALLOW is incorrect because it uses the port 22, which is the SSH port

Question 6 Answer: D

Since there are some 'write' requests possible, 'read' replicas will not work. Amazon Redshift is an OLAP database that will allow writes too.

Question 7 Answer: A, B,C

Question 8 Answer: A

Use AWS Lambda environment variables is the correct answer.

Question 9 Answer: D

Amazon79EFS is a fully-managed service that makes it easy to set up, scale, and cost-optimize file storage in the Amazon Cloud.

Question 10 Answer: A

In the Security Group, add an Inbound SSH

rule is the correct answer. To resolve the issue, you need to add an Inbound SSH rule.

Question 11 Answer:B

Envelope encryption is the correct answer.

Question 12 Answer: A

Redis is a cache engine that uses for complex data types.

Question 13 Answer: A

Replication is one of the best approaches in case of failure of the node; through this, you can quickly recover the data. It supports high availability, separates the 'read' and 'write' workloads. In Memcached, there is no redundancy of data, while in Redis, there is replication.

Question 14 Answer:C

When you need to distribute your data over multiple nodes, it is also useful in cases where you need to run large nodes with multiple cores and threads.

Question 15 Answer: 3

One is incorrect. You cannot enable encryption for an existing database.

Twoare incorrect. You cannot restore the encrypted snapshot to the existing database instance.

Three is correct. You need to take an encrypted snapshot and create a new database instance from the photo.

Analytics Answers

Question 1 answer: C

Amazon Data Pipeline: for running ETL jobs

Amazon S3: for storing large volumes of data

Amazon EMR: for running Hadoop

Amazon Redshift: for data warehouse

Question 2 answer(s): A, B,E

In production environments, other clones of ElastiCache and CloudFront can all help improve site performance. Changing the auto-scaling strategy will not help improve performance time because the performance problem is likely to be the back end of the database rather than the front end. Pre-configured IOPS is not helpful because the bottleneck is memory rather than storage.

Question 3 answer: A

You have the chance to enable static web site hosting for S3 buckets. It can do via the properties option for the bucket. The endpoint of the bucket for static hosting will also configure.

Question 4 answer(s):B

AWS RDS database not fully managesthe database; it partially manages. For RDS, we still need to specify the server capacity, security group, etc. It is the point most of them are confused because they assume that RDS is the fully managed database. Even though the question doesn't ask about the type of database (NoSQL), the correct option is DynamoDB. For the fully managed option, it is Aurora and DynamoDB. So, the right choice in this question is DynamoDB. The link provides the full details of the product.

Question 5 answer(s):D

AWS Documentation Reference:

AWS re:INVENT 2017: Analyzing Streaming Data in Real-Time with Amazon Kinesis

Ingest and deliver raw data

- CloudTrail provides continuous account activity logging

- Events sent in real-time to Kinesis Data Firehose or Streams

- Each event includes a timestamp, IAM user, AWS service name, API call, response, and more

Compute Operational Metrics in real-time

Amazon Kinesis data analytics compute metrics using SQL in real-time

Persist data for real-time dashboards

- Use Kinesis Data Firehose to archive processed to in S3

- Use AWS Lambda to deliver data to DynamoDB (or another database)

- Open source or other tools to visualize the data

Question 6answer:A, C, D, F

B and E are features of the EMR File System (EMRFS).

AWS Documentation Reference: Work with Storage and File Systems

Question 7answer:A,B

AWS Documentation Reference:

Whitepaper: Streaming Data Solutions on AWS with Amazon Kinesis

You use Kinesis Streams if you want to do some custom processing with streaming data.

Question 8 answer:A,D

You would either user EBS or EFS. S3 is for object storage, not applications, and Glacier is for data archiving.

Question 9 answer: B

Question 10answer:A

AWS   Documentation   Reference: Whitepaper:
Big_Data_Analytics_Options_on_AWS

Highly formatted canned Reports are not a scenario where Amazon Quicksight should uses.

Application Integration Answers

Question 1 Answer: 3, 5

Explanation:

The solutions architect must enable high availability for the architecture and ensure it is cost-effective. To help high availability, an Amazon EC2 Auto Scaling group should create to add and remove instances across multiple availability zones.

Question 2 Answer: 3

Explanation:

The Amazon EC2-based application must be highly available and elastically scalable. Auto Scaling can provide the elasticity by dynamically launching and terminating instances based on demand. It can take place across availability zones for high availability.

Incoming connections can distribute to the instances by using an Application Load Balancer (ALB).

Question 3 Answer: 3

Explanation:

AWS Batch Multi-node parallel jobs enable you to run single jobs that span multiple Amazon EC2 instances. With the help of AWS Batch multi-node similar jobs, you can run large-scale, tightly coupled high-performance computing applications and distributed GPU model training without directly starting, configuring, and managing Amazon EC2 resources.

AWS Batch multi-node parallel jobs are compatible with any framework supporting IP-based communication between nodes, such as Apache MXNet, TensorFlow, Caffe2, or Message Passing Interface (MPI).

Question 4 Answer: 3

Explanation:

Amazon CloudTrail can be used to log activity on the reports. The critical difference between the two answers that include CloudTrail is that one references data events, whereas the other references management events.

Question 5 Answer: 4

Explanation:

The application is writing the files using API calls, which means it will be compatible with Amazon S3, which uses a REST API. S3 is a massively scalable key-based object store that is well-suited to allowing concurrent access to the files from many instances.

Amazon S3 will also be the most cost-effective choice. A rough calculation using the AWS pricing calculator shows the cost differences between 1TB of storage on EBS, EFS, and S3 Standard.

Question 6 Answer: 3

Explanation:

This question is merely asking you to work out the best compute service for the stated requirements. The essential requirements are that the compute service should be suitable for a workload that can range quite broadly in demand from no requests too large bursts of traffic.

AWS Lambda is an ideal solution as you pay when requests make, and it can quickly scale to accommodate the large bursts in traffic. Lambda works well with both API Gateway and Amazon RDS.

Question 7 Answer: 3

Explanation:

You can use the CloudWatch agent to collect both system metrics and log files from Amazon EC2 instances and on-premises servers. The agent supports both Windows Server and Linux and enables you to select the metrics to be collected, including sub-resource metrics such as per-CPU core.

There is now a unified agent, and previously there were monitoring scripts. Both of these tools can capture SwapUtilization metrics and send them to CloudWatch. It is the best way to get memory utilization metrics from Amazon EC2 instances.

Question 8 Answer: 3

Explanation:

Amazon ElastiCache is an in-memory database. With ElastiCache Memcached, there is no data replication or high availability. The Redis engine must uses, which does support both data replication and clustering.

Question 9 Answer: 2,4

AWS Global Accelerator uses static IP addresses as fixed entry points for your application. You can migrate up to two /24 IPv4 address ranges and choose which /32 IP addresses to use when creating your accelerator.

This solution ensures the company can continue using the same IP addresses. They can direct traffic to the application endpoint in the AWS Region closest to the end-user.

Question 10 Answer: 1

Explanation:

The best option is to configure the database security group to allow traffic from the application security group. You can also define the destination port as the database port. This setup will allow any instance that is launched and attached to this security group to connect to the database.

Question 11Answer: 3

Explanation:

Amazon FSx for Windows File Server provides fully managed, highly reliable file storage accessible over the industry-standard Server Message Block (SMB) protocol. It is built on Windows Server, delivering a wide range of administrative features such as user quotas, end-user file restore, and Microsoft Active Directory (AD)

261

integration. It offers single-AZ and multi-AZ deployment options, fully managed backups, and encryption of data at rest and transit.

Question 12Answer: 2

Explanation:

CloudWatch Events rules can use to set automatic email notifications of medium to high severity results to an email address of your choice.You simply create an Amazon SNS topic and then associate it with an Amazon CloudWatch events rule.

Question 13 Answer: 2,4

Explanation:

None of the options present theright solution for specifying permissions required to write and modify objects. That requirement needs to be taken care of separately. The other conditions are to prevent accidental deletion and ensure that all versions of the document are available.

Question 14 Answer:2

Explanation:

The most cost-effective solution is to first store the data in S3 Standard-IA, where it will frequently access for the first three months. After three months expires, transition the data to S3 Glacier,storing at a lower cost for the remainder of the seven years. Expedited retrieval can bring retrieval times down to 1-5 minutes.

Question 15 Answer: 2

Explanation:

An Amazon Simple Queue Service (SQS) can be used to offload and decouple the long-running requests. They can then be processed asynchronously by separate EC2 instances. It is the best way to reduce the overall latency introduced by the long-running API call.

Question 16 Answer: 3

Explanation:

The Redis authentication token allows Redis to ask for permission (password) before allowing the client to execute commands, thereby improving data security. You can require users to enter a token on a Redis server protected by a receipt. For this reason, when creating a replication group or cluster, please include the parameter --auth-token (API: AuthToken) in the correct ticket. Besides, it should use in the replication group or all subsequent commands of the replication group.

CORRECT: "Redis AUTH command" is the right answer.

INCORRECT: "AWS Directory Service" is incorrect. It is a managed Microsoft Active Directory service and cannot add password protection to Redis.

INCORRECT: "AWS IAM Policy" is incorrect. You cannot use an IAM policy to enforce a password on Redis.

INCORRECT: "VPC Security Group" is wrong. A security group protects the network layer; it does not affect application authentication.

AWS Security, Identity & Compliance Answers

Question 1 answer:

Amazon Cognito manages authentication and authorization for your public-facing programs.

Question 2 answer:

The team members should place in groups as users with specific roles assigned to each of them, including the period of the day to access the platform.

Question 3 answer:

Amazon Web Services (AWS) should apply usage limits to most of its infrastructure and resources. But, users can request for such limitations to lift before accessing such services.

Question 4 answer:

Infrastructure as a service (IaaS) provides users access to the virtual components of a provider's physical resources. These customers handle their infrastructures the same way they would their physical servers.

Question 5 answer:

The method of authentication for accessing files is called access keys.

Question 6 answer:

The method of end-to-end encryption that protects data or files at every stage of its lifecycle is called client-side encryption.

Question 7 answer: 1

Explanation:

One is correct. The maximum filesize for Amazon S3 objects is five terabytes.

Twoare incorrect. It is the minimum file size possible in Amazon S3.

Three is incorrect. 5GB is not the maximum file size possible in Amazon S3.

Fourare incorrect. There is a limit on the maximum file size for objects in Amazon S3

Question 8 answer:

The main advantage of resource tags is to view and manage resources on active accounts, mainly if applied with consistent naming or descriptive patterns.

Question 9 Answer: 2

To specify permissions for a specific task on Amazon ECS, you should use IAM Roles for Tasks. The permissions policy can be applied to tasks when creating the task definition, or by using an IAM task role override using the AWS CLI or SDKs. The taskRoleArn parameter uses to specify the policy.

CORRECT: "Create an IAM policy with permissions to DynamoDB and assign It to a task using the taskRoleArn parameter" is the right answer.

Question 10 Answer: 1

Explanation:

You need to assign the role to the Lambda function, NOT to the DynamoDB table.

CORRECT: "Creating an Identity and Access Management (IAM) role with the required permissions to access DynamoDB tables and assigning the part to the Lambda function is the correct answer.

CPSIA information can be obtained
at www.ICGtesting.com
Printed in the USA
LVHW080913211220
674638LV00034B/107